Ad

"*A Mile Down* would be a cautionary ~~~~~~~~~~~~~~~ who dreams of the freedom of the high seas—if only it wasn't so damn exciting. David Vann takes us to exotic isles while bringing home the terrors of existential doubt and financial insecurity. He's asea in so many ways, yet steers the reader ably through the rocks and reefs of his own daunting problems."
— Stewart O'Nan, coauthor with Stephen King of *Faithful: Two Diehard Boston Red Sox Fans Chronicle the Historic 2004 Season* and author of *The Night Country*

"At once memoir, confession, travel book, and thriller, David Vann's *A Mile Down* is so vivid and intense you will dread to see it end. . . . The book is a testimony of passion and courage in deadly storms and scarier calms, of a man wrestling with his ghosts and gifts in the very shadow of paradise."
— Robert Morgan, author of *Gap Creek*

"*A Mile Down* is pure adrenaline. Vann by all rights should have died at sea, and yet he's lived to tell about it. But the thrill comes also from other kinds of risk—risk of repeating his father's suicide, risk of financial disaster, risk of prosecution, risk of losing everything including who he believes himself to be. This story won't let you go."
— Melanie Thernstrom, author of *The Dead Girl* and *Halfway Heaven*

"*A Mile Down* is far more than a tale of ruin at sea. It's also a story of desire and shame, of the struggle to escape our histories and know our dreams. Vann writes that 'A life can be like a work of art, constantly melted away and reshaped,' and he shows us this reshaping, this rebirth of hope from despair and ruin, so powerfully I couldn't put the book down. You have to read this book, even if you care nothing about sailing or the sea. Just read it."
— Lalita Tademy, author of *Cane River*

"*A Mile Down* is superbly crafted. As in the great epics, the protagonist faces an unrelenting crush of disasters, bad luck, and ill will, yet picks himself up over and over to carry on. And what shapes this struggle is the question of whether he is persisting through his own will or through obedience to a dead father who had similar struggles at sea. David Vann has created a tale of hubris and endurance that is both exciting and beautifully written."

—Keith Scribner, author of *The Goodlife* and *Miracle Girl*

"Riveting, heartbreaking, and redemptive . . . *A Mile Down* is a memoir as engaging as the most compelling of novels. . . . This is an immensely moving and exciting book—it's as if one of the heroes of *The Perfect Storm* had lived to write his memoirs."

—Julie Hilden, author of *3* and *The Bad Daughter*

"*A Mile Down* is mandatory reading for anyone who's ever flirted with thoughts of a life spent at sea."

—A. Manette Ansay, author of *Vinegar Hill*

"*A Mile Down* is a riveting and truthful account of a good man's attempt to stay afloat on treacherous waters. This book reminded me of Robert Stone's *Outerbridge Reach,* or John Casey's *Spartina,* but in many ways Vann's odyssey is more unforgettable. The fact that Vann lived to tell it is an achievement in itself."

—Tom Barbash, author of *The Last Good Chance* and *On Top of the World: Cantor Fitzgerald, Howard Lutnick, & 9/11: A Story of Loss & Renewal*

David Vann's work has been published in the *Atlantic Monthly* and other magazines and has won numerous awards. He has taught at Stanford and Cornell and currently teaches travel and adventure writing for a consortium of Oxford, Stanford, and Yale. He holds a U.S. Coast Guard 200-ton master's license and has sailed more than 40,000 miles offshore.

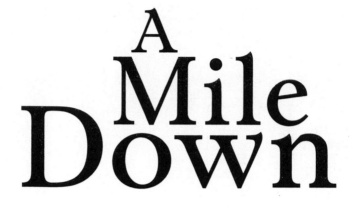

A Mile
Down

THE TRUE STORY OF
A DISASTROUS CAREER AT SEA

DAVID VANN

THUNDER'S MOUTH PRESS

NEW YORK

A MILE DOWN
THE TRUE STORY OF A DISASTROUS CAREER AT SEA

Published by
Thunder's Mouth Press
An Imprint of Avalon Publishing Group
245 West 17th Street, 11th Floor
New York, NY 10011

AVALON
publishing group incorporated

First printing June 2005

Library of Congress Cataloging-in-Publication Data is available.

ISBN: 1-56025-710-5

9 8 7 6 5 4 3 2

Book design by Jamie McNeely
Printed in the United States
Distributed by Publishers Group West

For my father, James Edwin Vann, 1940–1980

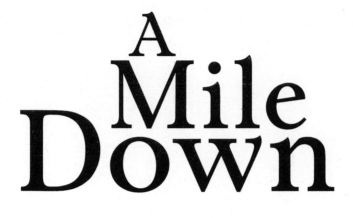

Part
One ⚓

THERE'S MORE ART in this world than we think. The art of welding, for instance. In the faint green light through the welding mask, the electrode in my right hand sends a funnel of energy shielded by inert gas, a miniature environment of purity, without the contamination of oxygen. At the melting point, the surfaces of the two aluminum plates form a molten crescent moon. With my left hand, I tap the end of an aluminum rod into the center of this moon and a new crescent instantly forms. Superheated, it sucks up into the sides of the plates and tugs at their edges, creating two small rivers and this vortex where I tap again, forming the newest moon. It's as beautiful as writing or love or anything else in this world, and it surprises me. I had imagined welding to be a brute task and nothing more.

The afterlife of ruin had seemed brutish, also. Sleepless nights, a general aching, and disbelief. But there were no recriminations from my wife or her family, and they gave me the room and support to recover, until new dreams arose and opportunities presented themselves. I've come to realize that a life can be like a work of art, constantly melted away and reshaped. This story is of that melting away.

In the summer of 1976, my father's new, sixty-three-foot aluminum commercial fishing boat was launched, and in the eight months of construction beforehand and the nine months of using the boat afterward, he must have experienced many of the very same vexations and dreams I was to experience building my own ninety-foot yacht in Turkey. I have thought more than once that perhaps I embarked on the entire boating enterprise simply to repeat his experience so that I could know him better—perhaps even, in a way, recover him after his death.

My father killed himself when I was thirteen, so my knowledge of him is limited. No one can tell me exactly why he decided to quit his dental practice and build a commercial fishing boat or what he felt when he had to sell the boat and return to dentistry.

His boat seemed a ship to me, grand and impossible. It was an adventure, and I do remember my father smiling, seeming happy, feeling the adventure as much as I did. I was too young to know anything of financial worries, but I like to believe my father was not thinking only of that. I like to think he enjoyed seeing the boat take shape, felt pleasure at running his hand along its raw aluminum hull that would never rust, not in a hundred years.

I remember how he looked then, too, very similar to how I looked when I was building my boat in Turkey. We were almost the same age, early thirties, both with the same short hair receding at the temples, both letting our beards grow a bit, both dressing in old T-shirts. And the oddity of what we were doing was remarkably similar. But I never consciously intended to repeat my father's life, only followed the opportunities I saw, and considering the complicated factors involved, it's just as easy to say the similarities occurred by chance.

• • •

I first visited Turkey and met Seref in the summer of 1997, just before running my first charters on a smaller boat in the San Juan Islands, north of Seattle. I was a lecturer at Stanford, teaching creative writing, and because it seemed I would not get a tenure-track job at any university—at least not until I published a book—I had started an educational charter business, earning my captain's license and teaching creative writing workshops aboard a sailboat. The workshops were offered through Stanford Continuing Studies. I was excited about the business and my new life as a charter captain, but when I visited Turkey that summer and saw the ninety-foot hull, my plans and dreams became much larger.

"I am Seref, pronounced like the good guy in one of your westerns," Seref told me. He was a handsome man in his early forties, wearing a polo shirt, shorts, and boat mocs. He owned a tourism agency on the Bodrum waterfront, and I was looking for someone to tell me about the large charter boats in the harbor. "I show you any of these boats," he said. "I am the president of the chamber of commerce in Bodrum. Everyone knows me."

I have loved boats all my life, gazed at all of them longingly, large and small, but I have never been so enchanted. These were enormous wooden sailboats, like pirate ships. Eighty feet long, some over a hundred feet, with bowsprits and wooden masts, varnished rails and carved sterns. On the bow of one of these, sailing along this coastline, I could imagine I was Odysseus, and in truth the boat he sailed on would have been almost the same in shape and material, different only in equipment.

The boats were made cheaply, however. In two of them, as I stood in their cabins, I could see sunlight through the walls.

Seref drove me along the sea to Icmeler, where the boats were made. On a wide dirt beach was a great crowd of wooden masts and hulls, most of them under construction, others hauled out for repair.

"We go to the yard that makes the steel boats," Seref said. "Boats that can go on any ocean."

We arrived at a warehouse with an overhead crane and two hulls being constructed beneath, one a traditional design, a gulet, but out of steel, the other probably a boat for dive charters, judging by its aft deck.

"This is my dive boat," Seref said. "It will be finished next month."

"Yours?" I asked.

"Yes, I know something about steel, David."

We moved on to the other section of the warehouse, which held one large steel hull. We stood beneath the stern. It was massive. MARCELLILLIAN was stenciled up high, temporarily. The boat had been named and registered but was sitting here unfinished except for the hull.

"This one I think is for sale," Seref said.

Grendel, my forty-eight-foot boat, was large, but this hull was on a different scale. Almost ten feet of draft for its twin keels. The rudder taller than I was, and broad, hung by a single stainless pole. Above this, another ten feet of freeboard to reach the deck; the boat stood over twenty feet above us and was just as wide. Two stories of boat. I asked its weight and length.

Seref said it was ninety feet. "And I don't know how many tons, but so heavy. Too heavy. Maybe 110 tons, I don't know."

Since I was already in debt with *Grendel,* I had no idea how I could possibly scrape together the financing. But I knew, as I stood there my first afternoon in Turkey, that even if it screwed up my life considerably, I was going to try.

I've always worked hard, but the idea of the working life has frightened me since childhood. I had nightmares of adults working hard and endlessly at tasks they did not enjoy so that they could continue working hard and endlessly at tasks they did not enjoy. There was no other purpose or end point. Work so that you can keep working. It seemed a proposition that could easily end in suicide. I wanted to escape this. I wanted to free myself from the working world and have time to write. And I wanted adventure. *Grendel* could never free me, but this boat could.

While I inspected the boat, Seref didn't say a lot. I think he knew, as good salesmen do, that I was already fashioning my own chains. There was no point in discussing anything practical. All that mattered was the dream. The dream of escape had me now, and everything else would be pulled along with it. I had no money at all, and it was impossible, but he must have known I had already bought this boat.

I leased a boat from Seref the following summer and ran charters along the Turkish coast. The ports we visited were ancient and gorgeous. I became good friends with some of the guests, and because *Avrasya,* the boat I had leased, was fully crewed, with captain, cook, and sailor, I was not responsible for maintenance or repairs or sailing the boat. I taught creative writing workshops morning and evening, enjoyed the tours with my guests, and had a glorious vacation all summer long.

My girlfriend, Nancy, joined me on several charters and for a three-week break between charters to travel through Greece and Italy. We had met at the Starlight Ballroom in the spring while I was still teaching at Stanford. It was drop-in night, and we happened to pick the same class. She was a beautiful Filipina with long dark hair and an easy laugh. As she switched partners around the circle, whoever she was with was laughing and showing off. I spoke with her briefly afterward, found out she was enrolling in swing and salsa, and signed up for the same classes. A few months later, we were touring the Mediterranean together on what felt like a honeymoon.

During these cruises, a curious thing happened: without quite meaning to, I sold loans for the new boat. I was simply telling my story to people who asked, but the story became a kind of spiel as I learned that these people—sometimes without my even asking—were willing to loan me money.

The questions came because the business was unique. But what interested these people, really, were dreams. I couldn't get a job as a professor, and I couldn't make any money as a writer, but instead of taking a job I didn't want, I was creating my own university on the water. It was an American Dream founded on another more recent dream, of continuing education, and my guests could feel satisfaction from participation in both. The two dreams fit together so well because really, in their best parts, they're the same dream. How many of us ever get the chance to live a life in which everything comes together perfectly, so that everything we do engages us and represents who we are?

By the end of the summer, I purchased the hull with loans from my guests. Seref and I tried to make a more detailed budget for finishing, but really there were too many unknowns. I would ship much of the equipment from the United States. The labor and wood and other basic materials were all cheaper in Turkey. Seref was going to put together a team of Bodrum's finest: the best electrician, carpenter, mechanic, and painter. He had the contacts, and this was a good, interesting boat, so he could get the best people, he said, and still keep the cost low. We would leave the boat in the yard's shed for three or four months, to lay the deck, paint the hull, finish the pilothouse, and install its windows, then the boat would be dragged outside and finished on the beach.

These were exciting times, making plans and walking through the enormous steel hull. I felt extremely lucky.

That fall and winter I kept raising loans and sending large amounts of money to Seref. Construction was fully underway. It was bothering me, though, that I couldn't be there, on site, to supervise. I was still teaching at Stanford fall and spring, and running charters on *Grendel* in Mexico during the winter.

Already it was seeming the boat would go over budget. Seref became cagey in February and March, no longer committing to stay within a certain range.

Then came the war in Kosovo. It filled the news all spring. As a result, Americans were not traveling to Turkey and no one was signing up for my charters. In addition to creative writing classes, I was offering great courses in classics and archaeology by professors from Stanford. The potential students— successful, intelligent professionals from the Bay Area and across the United States—told me again and again over the phone that the trips sounded wonderful and they would have signed up if not for the war.

I tried to point out that the war was not in Turkey, but in 1999, American geography lumped Turkey with all the other nameless countries around it, so no one cared. One woman, after receiving a postcard I had sent to five thousand people on the *Poets & Writers* mailing list, sent several notes cursing me for offering cruises in a place where warplanes were flying over every day and children were dying. I didn't know what to write back to her. That the warplanes she was thinking of were flying over Italy but not Turkey? That children are always dying in every country, but not currently in Turkey except from causes other than the war in Kosovo? Turkey has a million-man standing army. The idea that the ground war in Kosovo could have somehow spilled into Turkey was a bit imaginative.

The big political event for Turkey was the nabbing of the Kurdish rebel leader Ocalan (pronounced *Oh-je-lawn*) by the government. This triggered a U.S. State Department warning to travelers and also kept Americans away from Turkey, though it shouldn't have. Whether one considered Ocalan the true and persecuted leader of the Kurds in Turkey or simply a butcher and drug lord most Kurds didn't want any part of, either way his capture would lead to the most politically peaceful summer in Turkey in fifteen years.

Instead of making $200,000 in net income that summer, to help pay for the construction of the boat, I would take a loss. But every two weeks I still had to come up with another $25,000 or so for construction, and I didn't have any money. The boat was being financed through credit cards and loans from former passengers, and my reliance on credit cards was increasing. I was working hard at selling loans, but with Ocalan and Kosovo, they were getting harder to sell.

By the time I left again for Turkey, in early June 1999, after frantically reading and grading to finish teaching my four spring courses at Stanford, I was far behind financially. It was possible that construction would stop and the boat would not be launched. I was forced to cancel several empty charters to consolidate the summer and reduce my losses. Now my first charter wasn't until the end of July. But I wasn't sure the boat could be ready by then even if I came up with the money to keep construction going. I wasn't sleeping, and I was doubting myself, wondering why on earth I had ever decided to build this bigger boat. The weight of debt and failure seemed a physical thing lodged in my chest and far beyond my control.

The things I believed about myself were becoming untrue. I believed I always succeeded. I believed my hard work would pay off. I believed I was good for my word, that of course I would repay any debt. I believed I treated people well and fairly. I wanted to keep believing these things. And I knew my father had felt this same fear, of becoming something other than what he had always imagined himself to be. I wondered if this was part of what had made suicide begin to seem reasonable.

WHEN I ARRIVED in Turkey that June, the boat was down on the beach, among the great wooden hulls. Its masts lay alongside, one ninety feet long, the other sixty. I had chosen wood because it evokes the romance of sailing and the sea.

"I selected this wood myself," Seref said, a hand on the mainmast. "I let it dry for over two months. So strong."

I walked along the mast, happy to be with Seref again and happy to be in this beautiful place, on ancient shores. But the two men who were screwing aluminum sail track to its aft edge were not caulking. They were just putting the screws in dry, which would rot the wood. One of the two men had a bandage over his thumb, except that it ended short of where a thumb should be.

"What happened to his thumb?" I asked Seref.

"He lost it a few days ago working on some wood for the boat."

I looked again at the man and his bandage. This was terrible. I couldn't believe he had lost his thumb building my boat.

"He is clumsy," Seref said. "He already loses another finger building another boat. You don't need to worry about it. And he doesn't understand English, don't worry."

"But I have to do something." Though I couldn't think of what to do. It seemed so crass to give money. How does money replace a thumb? What I wanted was to make it not have happened.

"I already give him something," Seref said. "It is done. Don't think about it. Come." He gestured toward the other end of the mast. "We have to decide something."

I looked at the man again and nodded to him. "I'm sorry," I said. I felt like a monster. He had a face that didn't show anything to me, no remorse or pain or resentment or even recognition. If anything, he seemed impatient for me to leave so he could get back to work. I had no idea what to think or feel or do, so I turned and followed Seref.

The top of the mainmast had a stainless steel cap with a lot of wires and attachments.

"We have to decide this," Seref said. "You said you want battery cable to here, and a post for the lightning?"

"That's right," I said. "And a bonding plate below on one of the keels, and the grounds run to the hull. That way the lightning has a quick path to the water."

"Okay," he said. "You like your masts?"

"Well, they're not caulking the screws. And they're using two pieces of track, not one continuous piece, so every time I pull the sail down, it will get caught where the track is being joined. And the lower spreaders are supposed to have twin notches for the wires, not just one notch, and the ends of all the spreaders need boots. And the masts themselves are very heavy."

Seref smiled at me, then grabbed both of my shoulders. "David. I will say this to you. This boat is not finished. When it is finished, I will hand you the keys and everything will be done. Everything. Okay?" He let go of one of my shoulders and held an imaginary set of keys in the air.

I didn't believe him, but what could I say? I knew now I should have been working with a shipyard to finish the boat, not with the owner of a tour company, because at least some and perhaps all of the mistakes Seref was making were from lack of experience, not by design. But the summer before, when I had first bought the hull, I had believed, and Seref had encouraged me to believe, that he possessed the necessary experience and expertise and could finish the boat for less without the shipyard. Now he was doing his best, but his best might not be good enough, and it was too late for me to go with anyone else. I had given all of my money to Seref.

Seref led me up the ladder to see more. The deck was newly sanded, the space enormous, magnificent for sailing through the Mediterranean and across the Atlantic and Caribbean. The pilothouse was nearly finished. The dash under the forward windows, in mahogany strips caulked like decking, was varnished a deep, gleaming auburn.

"This looks great," I said, and Seref smiled and beckoned me below, down the companionway.

Below was a different story. I felt sick seeing it. The main salon and galley were bare steel. No deck, no walls, no ceiling, no galley partition or settee or desk. He hadn't done anything in here.

But Seref had already gone down the next set of stairs to the aft cabins, so I followed. Here, too, the floor was only steel, the ceilings bare with wires hanging. The walls for the hallway were tongue-and-groove mahogany, and the frames for the doors to the six aft staterooms had been fitted, but the wall going aft on the starboard side had a large bend to it. I was overwhelmed by disappointment and fear and could latch on to only this one detail. "This wall," I told Seref. "It isn't straight."

"It will be straightened," Seref said.

"When? I run a charter in six weeks. The wall has already been set. They're building the room onto it now."

"David. I said I would fix it. Now look at one of your staterooms."

I looked at one, and it was not what he had promised. It was solid mahogany, tongue-and-groove, as requested. But the strips of mahogany were greatly uneven. As I looked along any wall, I could see a strip of mahogany sticking out here and there. And it was all too late. The boat would have these imperfections until its final day. The boat had already gone far over budget, it still required more equipment and construction, and it was being built full of flaws.

I saw, too, that the insulation they were using behind the walls was only Styrofoam. They had just broken pieces of Styrofoam and stuck them in against the steel, then nailed the plywood over it. The corrosion would be a nightmare. In April, when I had visited for three days, I had asked for spray foam over all the steel before any wood was placed. That way the hull would last, would not rust from the inside.

"What about the spray foam?" I asked. "Where is the spray foam?"

"Yes, we need to talk about this. Now tell me what it is exactly that you want."

"But we've already talked about it, many times. And now it's too late. You can't spray anymore. You've already built over the steel." I turned away from Seref into one of the other rooms. I was not proud of myself, of how I was complaining, but nothing was right, and it was all too late.

I looked in one of the heads and saw that they were not finished either. Toilets still not installed, no sinks, no tile on the floor, walls unpainted. Eight of these bathrooms, one for each stateroom, and nothing had been done yet with any of them.

"We must talk about the bathrooms," Seref said. "What type of sinks you want. We will have to buy these. I have an idea, a good type of sink."

"Where are the toilets?" I asked. "The nine toilets that I

bought and sent clear back in December, half a year ago, $750 each, so they could be installed right away?"

"David, really you push too much. They are in the back rooms, the same as when you visited in April. We are waiting to decide on the floors first." He was looking out into the hallway. Many of the men were listening to us with one ear while they worked, some of them able to understand English, and I knew this bothered him.

"Well decide it now. Tile. Just put in some tile. White or green or whatever you can find. I have to run a charter in six weeks. You have to start deciding and working faster. You will not finish at this pace."

Seref put one hand through his hair and exhaled, then he walked out of the room. I was pissing him off, which was fine with me. It seemed necessary at this point.

I walked back through the bare main salon and down a hatch in the galley to the engine room. I found Ecrem in there with a shop light. I had met Ecrem in April, a small guy who looked almost English but spoke no English. He worked for very little money, Seref said, and he was doing most of the mechanical and plumbing work. We both smiled and nodded and said hello in Turkish. That was all we could do, so he went back to work, welding a platform for a discharge pump, sending white-blue light in jagged shapes along the steel walls. I could see myself outlined in these flashes like a burglar as I walked back between the engines.

I pulled out my flashlight. New diesels painted a dull blue. I traced their fuel lines and exhaust systems and found problems.

Seref called for me and I yelled I was in the engine room. I was going to tell him about the engines, but he came down the ladder with the electrician, a formal old man I had met in April who was reputed to be the best in Bodrum for a boat's electrical systems. He and Seref showed me the fuse box for the twenty-four-volt system, and I asked how the engine batteries tied in.

They looked puzzled and we went up to the electrical panels, which had been custom made in the United States and shipped to Turkey. Behind the panels were the big switches, and it was the cables to these I started tracing. They weren't run the way I had asked.

"These switches here," I showed both men, "in the emergency position, need to connect to the house banks."

The old man waved his finger back and forth, telling me no. He clucked with his tongue, as if I were an ignorant child. Then he talked to Seref in Turkish.

"He says they cannot connect to the house banks," Seref said. "He says the engines are only twelve volts and the house banks are twenty-four."

"What?" I asked.

Seref talked with the man again, then repeated the news to me.

"Seref, you told me the engines were twenty-four volt. I had the panels built, the switches ordered, and the entire system designed around twenty-four-volt engines."

Seref looked bewildered. "No," he said. "Just a moment."

He talked again with the man, who started gesturing. I didn't feel like waiting.

"What was he doing in putting together the whole wiring plan, Seref? None of it made any sense if the engines were twelve volt. What are these switches doing now?"

Seref put his hand up. "Calm down, David. Really. You mustn't talk like that. Really."

I tried not to get upset. I tried just to listen and explain. But none of this boded well at all.

"I don't know how he make this mistake," Seref said finally when the old man had gone. His hand was rubbing the top of his head. I decided to back off, but then I remembered the engines.

"We should talk about the engines, too, Seref."

"Ecrem is working on the engines. He will arrange all."

"There are no siphon breaks. The engines could be flooded

with salt water. They were supposed to be added by the yard before the boat was moved out here."

"They are coming, in the next week or two, they will do this. They know about this. They have not forgotten. Or I will have Ecrem do it. I take care of this. You don't worry. Come. We go." He walked up on deck and I followed. Before going down the ladder to the ground, though, I wanted to see the crew quarters. "Nothing has happened in the crew quarters," he said. "Let's go."

On the drive back to Bodrum, Seref did not want to speak to me. I looked out at the water passing, at the large boats, the new hotels, the bougainvillea and whitewashed patios, the castle on the point. This gorgeous place.

"I have a charter in six weeks," I said. "If everything is not done, and done right, I will fail, and then I will not bring more guests or build more boats. There will be no more business from me." Seref made a considerable amount from my guests, since he arranged hotels, cars, flights, and tours for them before and after my charters. He was receiving commissions from everything I spent, too. That's the system in Turkey. He never did admit to me that he was taking commissions every time we bought anything for the boat, but I was fairly certain he was.

"It is your first night in Bodrum," Seref said. "Have dinner with my family tonight. We will pick you up from your hotel at eight o'clock."

We didn't say anything more the rest of the drive. He dropped me off at a hotel that was not fancy, since I had asked for something cheap. I wanted to sleep on the boat but that would not be possible for some time, probably not until after launch.

The room was small, with bare dirty carpet, a small bathroom, and no air-conditioning. It was hot but I didn't care. I opened the window to a view of small houses on a hill, bright in the sunlight with white walls, red tile, and purple flowers.

I could hear the latest Cher song blasting from some corner club, "Do you believe in life after love, after love, after love, after love . . . ?" Nancy and I loved Turkey for its obnoxious waterfront clubs. I flopped down on the bed exhausted and set my alarm to sleep for two hours. In a few minutes, as I was drifting off, I heard the loudspeakers from the minarets start up from three mosques. The Arabic chanting over the pop music, the tones leading up toward Allah, the praise and sub-jugation in it and the sound, too, of bitterness and defeat, of human disappointment. Maybe I was making up that last part. I was still tired from the flights.

I awoke slowly, heavy with jet lag, and was whisked off to a magnificent garden with tables set beneath the trees. Seref's family was gathered at the bar, chatting with friends, and when we arrived, Seref's wife greeted me first. She was beau-tiful, with bright eyes and a genuine laugh.

"Welcome back to Bodrum," she said. "The lucky owner of a big new boat."

"Thank you," I said, then turned to greet the next and the next, all very friendly and kissing me on both cheeks. They really were a wonderful group of people, Seref's family and friends.

We sat at a long table for twelve and, without ordering, several large plates of *mezes* (appetizers) were passed around.

"I can't wait to run the charters," I said to Seref but really to the group. "All of the delicious mezes and other Turkish dishes."

"The cook, Muhsin, is very good," Seref said. "You will meet him tomorrow."

"I can't wait," I said. There were fifteen or twenty men working on the boat. One of them, Ercan, I recognized as one of my crew members. I had met him in April. The other two had signed on since then.

"I must give a toast," Seref said. He picked up his wineglass and we all picked up ours. "To David, who is very special to me. With him I am building not only a beautiful boat but also a lasting friendship."

Seref's charm was hard to resist. I thanked him and we all clinked and drank. I began talking then with Nazim, Seref's best friend, sitting beside me. He spoke very good English and was a pleasant man. He had long curly hair and round glasses, like a rock star. He was the Camel cigarette distributor for the Bodrum area and smoked like a fiend.

"Your boat," he said. "People are talking about it. They say it will be worth a million dollars when it is finished."

Despite what I had originally hoped, there was no universe in which the boat was worth a million, especially here in Turkey. Still, I didn't want to sound nasty. "Well," I said. "It isn't finished yet."

"Yes, I know, but it will be finished. Seref is building this boat for you like it is his own boat. He goes to it every day since the winter, and he is trying to make everything perfect."

I studied Nazim. He seemed genuine. He seemed to believe what he was saying, and it really was possible he did believe. It was even possible that Seref believed he was building the boat as if it were his own. This was what frustrated me about doing business in Turkey. I couldn't know what to believe. Had Seref purposely ignored many of my requests and allowed shoddy work because he knew he could get away with it, because my time and finances were limited and I would have no legal recourse here in Turkey? Had he lied to me from the first about the cost of the boat, and was he putting the screws to me now because I was trapped and he thought I could raise more money? I knew the original purchase of the hull and engines had been a bargain, but I couldn't be certain of anything that had happened since.

"I know Seref is doing everything he can for the boat," I said. "And I'm grateful. But I'm still worried we won't be ready on time."

"Have faith, my friend. I have known Seref a very long time. He will come through with what he has promised."

I decided this man just didn't know. He probably did believe Seref was doing his best. Or he was planted next to me at this dinner table to brainwash me. It didn't change anything, either way. "Let's drink to that," I said.

After dinner, I walked down to the harbor, which is magical at night. Hundreds of wooden masts and carved sterns, the peninsula on the southern side with its maze of restaurants, shops, and clubs. The castle, its walls lit, defending the entrance and the bay. A true medieval castle, intact with its towers from the crusades, one for the French, one for the English, one for the Germans, etc.; each of the European nations warring in the name of Christianity stayed here and kept building. No major battles, except among themselves. At one point some treachery in which dozens were killed by their own and buried in a common grave. When the castle at Rhodes finally fell, they scampered away without a fight. The only bombardment came in World War I from a French ship. Then it became a prison. Now it's a museum, specializing in underwater archaeology, and flies a Turkish flag. We live in better times than most.

The phones lined up near the base of this castle rarely work. I went down the line of them inserting my card and found a working one on the fifth try. I called Amber first. She was running the business from our new, cheap office space in Menlo Park, California, and would have messages and bills and problems for me. Because of the travel, it had been two days since I had checked in.

As it turned out, though, Amber did not have the list of bills together. She promised she would put it together in an e-mail and I'd have it the next morning. She didn't have any new clients, no trips sold. She hadn't been doing any callbacks, either. She was somewhat busy with her own life, it seemed, and not at all apologetic about it. She also hadn't updated the Web site with any of the new course information or itineraries for our winter offerings in Mexico.

"So any news from any potential lenders?" I asked.

"I talked with John. He's still going to give us the loan."

I only had to make it until October, four months away, when John, who was one of my lenders and Amber's former fiancé, would inherit half of his $7 million from his father on his twenty-fifth birthday and give me a loan for $150,000, which would bail me out.

I called Nancy next, a much more pleasant call. Though I had been gone for only two days, I already missed her. We had been together for a year, and I was used to seeing her every day. It was possible we might marry, so I couldn't help but wonder if it was her future now, too, that might be collapsing.

BEING A FOREIGNER reshapes you. You feel born again into the world. I was no longer a teacher at Stanford, a California resident, a local. I was the captain and owner of a ninety-foot yacht being built by the Turks on the shores of the Aegean. This, combined with the fact that I was on the edge of ruin and under extreme time pressure, was an interesting feeling.

When I walked into the Borda office, Seref at his desk in the back was freshly showered and his hair neatly combed. He wore a polo shirt, shorts, boat mocs, an expensive watch, and sunglasses hooked into the front of his shirt. He was always like this, no matter how busy things were. I always felt like an American slob, and I also felt genuine affection for him. I liked this man. I think he liked me, too, despite the difficulties. I was hoping today would be better than yesterday.

"Good morning, my friend," he said.

"*Gun ayden*," I said. Turkish is a completely foreign language, with no cognates. *Gun* means *day*, not *good*.

"Have you had breakfast?" He pointed to an opened white paper package of my favorite Turkish breakfast treat, pastry dough in many layers filled with potatoes cooked in some delicious sauce similar to curry.

"I love these," I said.

"You are welcome, my friend. Have what you like, and then we will talk."

Turks and Europeans and maybe all other people in the world are better than Americans about not polluting every moment with business. They take pauses, no matter what's going on. In the States, I would have been chewing and talking at the same time, being efficient, but I appreciated that here I could take a few minutes to enjoy my breakfast.

The other people in Seref's office were friendly. The travel arrangements for my guests would be arranged by Ugur, who introduced himself to me. His name was difficult for me to pronounce, like *ooh-er* but with something else going on with the *g*. He was in his mid-thirties, balding, and cheery.

"How's business this summer?" I asked him while I ate my breakfast, breaking the rule without even thinking.

"It's terrible," he said. "Really terrible. This Ocalan problem is a big problem for Turkey."

"It's been going on since 1984 or 1985, right?"

"Yes, many years, but now they catch him. Your government and Israel government help. I am Kurdish, but I would like to kill this man. He end all business. This summer finished."

I didn't know what to say. It was a sensitive subject, and I didn't know much about it. I had done some research online, since the capture of Ocalan was screwing up sales for my charters and people were asking me about him, and from everything I could find, it seemed he was a butcher and a criminal, not a political leader deserving any sympathy. It was true the Turks had been barbaric to the Kurds, but Ocalan wasn't just leading his people out of this oppression. He was trafficking in arms and drugs, and he was slaughtering a lot of innocent people, including Kurds. He had murdered Kurdish teachers in eastern Turkey, for instance, because they were teaching Turkish to Kurdish children. A desire to preserve his language and culture was laudable, but murdering Kurdish teachers made me think he should swing. The best option, of course, was what the Turkish government was doing, which was to keep him behind bars and never kill him, so they had a hostage to help prevent further terrorism by Ocalan's organization. I wasn't going to say any of this out loud in Turkey, however, because it was possible I was wrong, and it might not matter whether I was wrong or right. Someone might take offense regardless. "Huh," I finally said. That seemed noncommittal enough. Just another American who didn't read the news.

"Really I would like to kill him," Ugur said.

I wiped my hands on a napkin and nodded to Seref. "Well, it's nice meeting you," I said to Ugur.

"Nice to meet you," he said.

I sat down opposite Seref, and he opened a folder that had printouts of e-mails from me, faxed plans for the electrical system, receipts, etc.

"Now, we need another transfer," Seref said. "I make these men wait, because I can. I know them many years. But they need to have their money now. Also, we need much equipment. We need tiles for the bathrooms, sinks, some marble for the galley, all the cushions need to be made now. The cushions we make with a good friend of mine, he say he begins right away, but still is necessary two or three weeks. This boat take a lot of cushions. Seventeen beds, one sitting area inside, five big sitting areas outside." Seref puffed his cheeks a bit. "This is many things. And many other things, too. Everything for the galley, we need to buy this. I know a place here in Bodrum. And the floors. We have to decide wood or carpet."

"I want wood," I said. "Carpet gets wet and mildews."

"But what type of wood? Wood is expensive, it takes time."

"I know," I said. "But I really don't want carpet, as I said before, when we talked last summer."

"Okay." He nodded his head.

We went through many other items, from pots and pans to blankets and anchors. A boat is made up of literally thousands of items, most of them special-purpose or oddly shaped. We still had pumps to get, plumbing and electrical decisions to make, the layout of the main salon to design. It was truly overwhelming. If I'd had more money and hadn't had any charters scheduled for that summer, it wouldn't have been difficult. But on a tight budget and time schedule . . .

"We go," Seref finally said, and we drove out to Icmeler, to the boat. This would become our daily routine. I'd meet Seref in his office for breakfast and talk about finances and construction plans, then we'd drive out to the boat to discuss issues and oversee the work, then we'd run errands around town, trying to buy the various things we needed, then back to the boat to deal with more problems. In the evening, I'd go to the phones and Internet cafés to get loans and sell trips and try to hold my business together.

At the boat that day, I met the crew. Ercan (pronounced *Air-John*) I had met before. He was strong, about my height, same age (thirty-two), dark-skinned, his head nearly shaved. He had a reputation for being a hard worker and a competent captain. The cook, Muhsin, was in his forties. He was a big guy who wore overalls and a baseball cap and smoked even more than the others, if that was possible. He spoke English fairly well and would be my interpreter for the other two crew. The sailor was Baresh, only seventeen years old. He was a kid. Small and wiry, handsome. He was friendly but didn't speak any English. Seref said he was taking the kid on as a favor to his mother, a family friend, but he thought Baresh would be good crew.

There were at least a dozen other men working on the boat at all times, mostly on carpentry but also painters, electricians, and the mechanic, Ecrem. It felt odd to be the owner, the client, walking around the boat inspecting, checking the work of sometimes up to twenty-five men. I felt like a boss, the über boss, above Seref. But that was only for a few moments. Mostly I felt helpless, because I kept finding new problems and there wasn't time or money to fix them.

The environment inside the boat was smoke and sawdust and the whine of saws and other power tools, everyone puffing away as they worked. I was especially interested in the head carpenter, a thin, homely guy who had a quick smile and was very traditional. He was one of only two or three who followed the call to prayer during the workday, spreading out a small, rough carpet inside whatever state-room he was working on and doing his prostrations and prayers. He was not a good carpenter at all by American standards, but he seemed like a good and honest man, full of jokes and songs and obviously liked by the other men. I liked his songs especially—when I could hear them over the table saws and drills. Traditional songs, his voice wavering up high, full of melancholy. The others quiet in their work when he sang. The sound of tools, but no talking. Occasionally one or two would join in. His songs were of a world I had never inhabited. Listening to him, I could forget, for a few minutes at least, all my worry. I was in a foreign land, with all that is rich and good about that.

The men took an afternoon break for tea at about four o'clock. They would gather out in the pilothouse and a boy would come from one of the shipyard kitchens with the tradi-tional pot and small glasses. The men put sugar cubes in and stirred with tiny spoons. They relaxed and chatted, the car-penter frequently telling jokes. I couldn't understand any-thing they were saying, but I liked the atmosphere. They were laborers and poor, but they seemed more European than third world. They looked aft to the sea and one of the islands, lovely in late afternoon, and they seemed part of an older culture.

Constantinople had been the height of Western civilization for five hundred years, and that fact had not been forgotten.

I visited many small vendors and shops with Seref, some right up from the beach, next to the boat. The teak lattice for the bowsprit was being made in a shop a hundred yards away.

Next door was the shop for stainless steel, which the Turks call *inox*. The man here was young and skilled, making all custom fittings. I explained and sketched the various pieces I would need for the rigging, including many items he had never seen before. Winches mounted on stainless bands around the masts so that no screws went into the wood. Angled mounts for rope clutches so that a single winch could manage four lines.

Most of the shops Seref and I visited were in Bodrum. The carpenter's shop was high up on a hill above town, and we went there many times, sometimes early in the morning to pick up the crew of carpenters and lumber. The place was more like a den. We had to walk down from the dirt road into a basement, where the shop stretched through four or five large, dark rooms. Enormous tools for milling. They were making everything from scratch out of logs Seref had purchased.

As Seref talked with the carpenters I saw boards planed and sawed, grooves cut, plugs drilled. The one thing I did not see was a lot of sanding. Everything was rough cut and then delivered to the boat, where it was installed. The lack of sanding was beginning to annoy me. They had already varnished some parts of the boat that hadn't been thoroughly sanded. I could see chatter marks and valleys in what should have been smooth, hard, level surfaces. Seref's response was always "All will be fixed. All will be ready when the boat is finished. I will take care of all," so I wasn't prevailing. It was hard to ask for rushed construction and careful construction at the same time.

My favorite place was the marble yard. When we first visited, it looked like a new, fresh, unfinished graveyard, with slabs of marble propped up everywhere but not engraved. As we walked to the office we passed an open-air shop with only a roof and three walls. Two men were cutting marble, and I was startled by them. They came up to shake Seref's hand and then mine, and they looked identical. They were entirely white from the dust, from their shoes up to their curly hair and beautiful faces. They were brothers—twins, I finally realized. They had perfect Mediterranean features, with full lips and sculpted noses and brows. Their curly hair must have been dark but was now white, pure white from the dust of marble, which is unlike any other dust. They looked like statues. Twin brothers metamorphosed into marble after running from something—a terrible father, perhaps. They were worthy of myth. I stared. I couldn't help it. They were perhaps the most wonderful and strange vision I had ever seen.

Seref pulled me away into the office, where we sat with a grimy old Turk who fought over price, but my mind was still back with the mythic brothers. I found it hard to care about the price or the thickness of the counter or the diameter of the two rounded sinks.

In the evenings, when I left Seref and the boat and all the shops and oddities, I stood again under the minaret and Bodrum castle making my calls, and I tried to express some of what I had seen to Nancy. Our calls were too short, because the cost was too high, but I wanted to share some of this experience. I was falling in love with Turkey, despite the frustrations and fears. No matter how the boat turned out, this was a magical place and I was grateful for my time here, to be seeing this.

Nancy was anxious to join me. She had visited Turkey the previous summer for only two charters and a few days afterward, but in those last few days we had toured the new route through ancient Lycia. Seref had driven us farther south along the coast. We saw towns and coves from Gocek to Antalya, so we knew it was going to be even better than ancient Caria.

The ruins, especially, would be much more numerous, older and more ornate, and better preserved. Nancy and I wanted the charters to begin.

The trips weren't selling, however. I had maintained hope that maybe we'd have some last-minute enrollment from people who saw that the war in Kosovo hadn't in fact spilled over into Turkey and Ocalan's supporters hadn't unleashed massive terrorist attacks. But no one was signing up. The few trips I was going to run would be at a loss, and though I dearly wanted to just cancel all of them, I couldn't. I had professors coming. The Homer's *Odyssey* course had a few students, so at least that trip would go off well, but the archaeology course had only two students. And a famous, extremely well liked professor. It was going to be embarrassing.

My first summer in the San Juans, I had easily filled eight weeks. The summer of 1998, in Turkey, had been even more successful, with many repeat customers. I had also run winter trips in the Virgin Islands and the Sea of Cortez. And this summer I was offering a better route, a better boat, better course offerings, famous and accomplished teachers, and reduced prices, and still no one was coming. I didn't see how I was going to make it. I was fighting over the construction of the boat all day, every day, trying to get it finished and launched on time, but this also meant I was spending money I didn't have, and my credit was about to end.

Seref and I fought over so many items partially because of what he himself called his Black Sea mentality. "I come from the Black Sea," he said. "And there, we don't have a lot of money, but we find a way."

His resourcefulness was admirable, and very much in line with my own attempts to save money, but it also meant storing the propane tank down in the galley next to the stove, for instance, even though it was an explosion hazard. I wanted a box on deck, vented so the fumes couldn't collect in any enclosed portion of the boat.

"This is not necessary, David," he said. "All these boats here use this system."

I hated to sound like a jerk, but his explanation didn't matter. "I don't care if these other boats want to blow up," I said.

"None of these boats blow up. You do not know this system."

"Seref. Propane is heavier than air and can ignite from a spark after collecting in any enclosed space. No amount of tradition can change science."

So Seref took the tack he usually did when he hit a wall, which was to argue that even if I wanted this change, it wasn't possible in the design and with how much time we had. It was the same approach he took with the anchor and the exhausts for the engines and various other items.

"Where does this tank go?" he asked. "There is no place for it out there."

So the days ground on, filled with anger and disappointment, and if I had had a way out of the whole business, I would have taken it. But the owners before me had spent $250,000 and received only $100,000 of the $140,000 I had paid. That's what happens when you try to sell a boat that is still under construction. You lose a lot of money. I was locked into finishing and then using the boat successfully. That was the only way I would be able to pay everyone back.

LAUNCH DAY FINALLY arrived. Traditionally, we should have been sacrificing an animal—a goat, I think. But I said no. I was also supposed to give big tips to everyone, for luck, but I didn't have the money. I walked around the boat with Nancy and wished we'd had more time. It would have been better to complete everything before launching.

I kept staring at the name on the stern. It had been a lovely gift from Seref, a varnished wooden plaque carved by a friend of his in Bodrum, but I worried that all of its bolts through the steel would cause corrosion.

The name itself was odd, too: *The Wife of Bath*. My company was Canterbury Sails, offering educational pilgrimages, as it were, beginning with writing workshops. But no one understood the name, especially in foreign countries. My Turkish crew couldn't even pronounce it. And I wasn't sure the sign was lined up quite right. It was hard to tell. The sun was very bright off the white hull.

The boat would be pulled backward into the water on large

wooden skids. It was an old system, with cables attached fore and aft. Planks were laid out behind the boat like railroad ties for the skids to slide over.

"We use this system for hundreds of years," Seref said. "Not with steel cable or tractor, of course. But this is same system."

"It's the system the Easter Islanders used to move around those huge statues," I said. "At least according to one theory. But other scientists say the system couldn't have worked, that the statues would have fallen off."

Seref shook his head and smiled. "You think like no other person," he said. Then he patted my shoulder and walked away.

By around noon, the yard crew was finally ready, and the tractor, revving up, started pulling. There were shouts immediately, then readjustments to the skids, then movement again. The whole thing looked dangerously top-heavy, but the skids moved smoothly over the ties, and after about fifty feet, the stern hanging over the edge of the water, the tractor eased up and the boat stopped.

I was inspecting the cable system. It was anchored ahead of where the bow had been, and had a brake on it, using blocks. Seref told me the next step would be to ease the boat toward the water, then let it go so that it slid back without tipping over. If they hit the brakes once it was back at an angle, it would fall onto the stern. So they had to let it glide at the end.

"I'm very nervous about this," I said. "The launch basically is not controlled. Has a boat ever fallen over backward or sideways?"

"David, really you worry too much. This happen maybe once or twice. But almost all the time the boat just glide into the sea."

We would be up on deck when the boat was let go. Seref and Nancy and I, and the crew. So at least Seref was risking his own life. I asked him whether our Turkish insurance policy would cover an accident at launch, and he said it would. And there was no other solution. I couldn't make a 150-ton travelift suddenly appear.

After various final preparations had been made, about ten people were up on deck and I was down in the bilges, checking. In the engine room I found Ecrem not doing anything about two large holes in the side of the hull. They were going to be exhausts for the generator and one of the discharge pumps; the holes were about three inches in diameter. I tried to motion for him to close them, using made-up sign language, since he didn't speak English and I didn't speak Turkish. Finally I had to yell for Seref, and he came down to interpret.

"Please tell him to close these holes," I said.

Seref talked with him and then said, "He can't close them. These exhausts will not have valves. The hoses will fit over the pipe."

"Well we can't launch with them open."

Seref talked with Ecrem again. "He says they are above the waterline."

"When we go flying back into the water, the water is going to slosh a bit, don't you think?"

"Okay, David, okay," Seref said. "I tell him to close this."

"Thanks," I said. Then I went through the rest of the engine checks while he talked more with Ecrem. I made sure the engine intake valves, diesel lines, and shaft gland cooling valves were open. This way of launching was difficult for me to accept. We'd hit the water at speed, drifting around uncontrolled and banging into other boats if we couldn't start our engines. I knew I shouldn't make comparisons, but in the U.S. this would never happen. On a railway or a travelift, engines are started and tested with the boat fully afloat, before the lines are cast off. I didn't like my options here because I didn't have any.

When I had checked everything and was back on deck, I made sure the rudder was centered and then stood at the helm, ready with the ignition switches, and asked Seref to give the order.

Seref yelled, and Nancy looked at me with fear. We were twenty-five feet off the ground, on a hundred-ton, top-heavy steel boat on thin wooden skids sliding backward without any brakes. I had no idea what was going to happen.

At first, nothing happened. Then we began moving, slowly. Then we were moving backward quickly, a feeling of enormous weight and power released. The fall was extremely far. I clung to the helm and hoped.

A huge sound of water rushing and we were in. We hadn't tipped over. But we were still moving fast, and starting to curve back toward shore. I hit the ignition buttons for both diesels and they roared to life. I looked at the depth—fifteen feet, only about six feet of water beneath our keels. A lot of people were yelling, telling me to do all kinds of things. I looked around for other boats. I put one of the engines in forward to slow our speed and spun the helm to bring the bow around.

Something was wrong, though. We weren't slowing down much. I gave it more power, and we didn't seem to slow at all. There were two small boats anchored in our path behind us. Seref pushed me aside and grabbed the throttles, but he became confused, too, and was using the throttles and wheel randomly. He was lost. Then Ercan pushed him aside and the three of us fought for the wheel.

"Stop!" I yelled. "Something's wrong with the props or engines. They aren't responding correctly."

"I drive," Ercan said. "I am captain."

"I'm the captain," I told him. "Get away from the helm. Both of you."

We were close to the boats, bearing down on them, completely out of control. Then I figured it out. The throttle was backward. Ecrem had mounted it backward, so that when we hit forward, we were really hitting reverse. I put the throttles in reverse (which was forward), spun to avoid the boats, and got us into deeper water.

"Seref," I said. "We almost ran over those boats and went aground."

"I don't understand how Ecrem do this," he said.

Then I gave him the helm, asked him to steer straight at low speed, and went below to check for water.

I found Ecrem just holding on, not doing anything. The two holes were not plugged. They were showing sunlight and I could see that the hull was wet below them. I pointed at the holes and yelled at Ecrem, but just then Seref revved the engines, which was deafening, and threw the boat into a sharp turn. This put the holes underwater. Two thick streams poured in, then stopped as we rolled to starboard, then poured in again as we rolled back. Ecrem pulled his shirt off and stuffed it into one of the holes, holding his hand over the other. I took off my own shirt and stuffed it into the other hole.

I left Ecrem with the shirts and returned to the pilothouse. "What are you doing?" I asked Seref. "I said go straight, at slow speed. There's water pouring in down there because Ecrem didn't bother to plug the holes and you just had to do some circles."

"Water? In the boat? Where is this water?"

On our way to Bodrum harbor, Seref made me pose for a photo with him on the aft deck, shaking hands. Our launch photo. It was silly, but he insisted, so I put on another shirt and smiled and posed. Then I went forward to the bow with Nancy to take a few deep breaths. It was a sunny, calm, perfect day, Bodrum castle coming closer off to starboard.

"I hope this works out," I said.

"Everything will get better," Nancy said.

But things did not get better. Later in the day, when we were moored in the Bodrum fleet and one of the boats asked us to adjust our position, I tried starting my engines and nothing happened.

Seref asked Ecrem to figure it out, but I said no. I wanted someone other than Ecrem. So Seref called Ecrem's brother, the "master" mechanic. He was supposed to be the best in Bodrum. And when he arrived, he was at least bigger and older than Ecrem. Literally twice his size. He went down to the engines while Ercan hit the starters from above, and he said immediately that there was salt water in the engines. It had flooded in through the exhausts because the siphon breaks hadn't been run correctly.

Seref translated this for me reluctantly. I couldn't believe I was hearing it. I had told Seref over and over how important the siphon breaks were, and he had reassured me they were correct.

Seref could see that I was losing it so he put his hands up and tried to calm me. "I don't know how this happen, David."

"Now you've destroyed my new engines," I yelled. I just couldn't keep from yelling. "Seventeen thousand dollars for each engine, and you've filled them with salt water. How many goddamn times did I tell you to make sure the siphon breaks were right? I'm not a mechanic, I don't know how they're supposed to be run, but I told you over and over how important they are."

Though I shouldn't have lost it, all of these things were in fact true. It was very frustrating, especially after the other events of the day. At first Seref yelled back at me, but finally he gave up and left.

I stayed in the engine room with the mechanic and helped him drain thick white soup from the oil pan. Then we removed the injectors and cranked each engine with a bar on the flywheel to pump out white froth at high pressure. It went all over the engine room. I didn't even care about the mess. Salt water in the engines was the worst possible thing we could do to them, and I'd need to rely on these engines for years. I was aware that I had behaved like a child, screaming like that, but I was so afraid. I had borrowed so much money for this boat. I had no safety net.

• • •

For the next twelve days, I was at the boat from 7 A.M. until midnight. We finished the bathrooms with white and green tile, household-style toilets, and even a bit of varnished trim on the cabinet doors. I was pleased with how they turned out.

For the floors in the staterooms and hallways, Seref found some cheap wood laminate. He didn't consult with me beforehand. I came up on deck one afternoon, after working in the engine room, and found a huge pile of the stuff already brought on board. I didn't have time to fight for anything else.

Seref and I didn't exactly make peace after the incident with the engines. We just moved on. There was too much to do. We spent a lot of time with the young guy who was building the air-conditioning units. We weren't going to have them for the first charter, but he would meet us in Gocek and install them in the twenty-four hours between charters.

The ceilings took more time than I would have thought. Seref cut shallow grooves in cheap, quarter-inch ply to mimic planking. This was inserted between braces in each ceiling section, then painted white, and it actually looked good. The contrast between the dark varnished mahogany beams and the white planked spaces looked rich. No one would ever know.

The compass I had shipped from the States was broken, and because it was specialized, with magnetic arms to compensate for the steel hull, I was unable to find a replacement. I would have to order another one, which meant I would have no compass for this twenty-four-hour trip to Antalya and the first few charters, perhaps even the entire summer. The Turkish crew was nervous about this. They had never been underway at night, or for twenty-four hours nonstop, and now they would have to do it without a compass. They told me it couldn't be done.

"Relax," I told them. "It sucks, but a compass isn't necessary."

At the end of our twelve days in Bodrum harbor, we had a long list of unfinished items. Seref would bring a construction crew to Gocek. But for now, at least we were seaworthy and the systems were running.

When we cast off, the other crews in the fleet were happy to see us go. We had been an inconvenience, and everyone knew we weren't Turkish-flagged, either, and shouldn't have been allowed here. We left feeling remarkably relieved. The worst part was behind us.

THE MEDITERRANEAN WAS like a lake, almost flat calm, the moonlight reflected in thousands of tiny crescents. And it was warm. No other boats whatsoever. Not one other boat sailing or motoring at night on that entire coast.

As daybreak neared so did the land and with first light we could see mountains. The Turkish crew were able to steer again. I tried to point out that, in terms of a visual reference, having a mountain off the port bow was really no different than having the moon or stars off the port bow, but they weren't convinced. They resented not having a compass.

The sunrise was spectacular, coming up pink and orange just as we passed between tall cliffs on the port side and a jagged island to starboard, with pinnacles before and after. The gap was narrow, only about a hundred feet. I woke Nancy and she came up to see. We went to the bow, to the teak platform above the bowsprit. We were gliding above glassy, pink water, the cliffs and island pink rock dotted with olive trees, the air warm. This was paradise.

We arrived in a harbor outside Antalya at about 9 A.M. By the time my lone passenger arrived in his taxi, we had the boarding ladder down and the salt washed off the boat, everything clean and ready. Our first charter. It felt so disappointing to run the first charter for one person, but I couldn't cancel because it was a new course for Stanford Summer Session, offering undergraduate units, and at least Kevin was a former student of mine and completely likeable. He was extremely bright, charming, and well traveled for a twenty-year-old. He had spent a lot of time in Yemen, and as we sailed back along the coast toward our first anchorage, he told great stories about the tall, skinny houses and the drug that everyone smokes. Apparently the entire country is hooked on a local drug that the rest of the world isn't interested in. So nothing ever really gets done in Yemen, and the land is still divided into tribal territories. To cross the country, you have to meet with each local tribal chief to pass through his land.

Nancy and I were excited because this was a new part of the coast for us. We were going to anchor in a tiny bay we'd heard about just west of the ruins of Olympos. We went forward to the bow with Kevin while Ercan steered and Muhsin and Baresh prepared lunch. We chatted and laughed, and it felt as if the good part of the summer was beginning, the good part, even, of our lives. We had many years in beautiful places to look forward to, with smart and interesting guests.

Our anchorage was magnificent. Steep mountains on either side, two small islands at the narrow entrance, and a low saddle beyond the inside shore, leading to another lovely bay. No habitations, no other boats, just this amazing place all to ourselves. We dropped anchor in the center and I backed within about thirty feet of a white cliff, then Baresh jumped into the water with our stern line tied around his waist. He climbed to an outcropping, tied us off, and dove back in. It all went very smoothly.

Because of Kevin's good company, the ease of running a

charter for one guest, and the spectacular coves and ruins, this charter was almost entirely a pleasure. There were some problems developing with the boat, however. The caulking on deck was coming loose, for instance. Within a week, there was one section on the starboard side, near the boarding ladder, that I could actually pull out for almost a foot.

Grendel's deck caulking was twenty years old and showed no signs of this. One afternoon Ercan and I inspected the deck thoroughly and found loose seams from the bow all the way back to the poop deck on the stern. It was all coming up.

I waited until Nancy and Kevin went for a paddle in the kayaks and called Seref on Ercan's cell phone.

Seref didn't want to believe it. "This cannot be true," he said. "There is some other problem. The Cekomastik does not come up like this."

I asked Seref to replace the seams in Gocek, between charters, and this became a daily fight over the phone, without progress. He had the advantage of time. If he delayed long enough on anything he didn't want to do or didn't want to do my way, I'd have to accept his solution in the end, because I had these charters to run and then I was leaving for Mexico.

We arrived in Gocek at the end of our first charter, said goodbye to Kevin, and greeted Seref and the construction crew. They had brought a lot of materials and equipment with them, including the AC units, the roller-furling and sail, and the marine plywood and mahogany, but they hadn't brought anything to recaulk the deck.

I pulled Seref aside to walk down the dock while the men unloaded everything. The waterfront in Gocek is lovely, the small town tucked into the head of a large bay with dozens of forested islands and a mountain rising directly behind it. The late morning was sunny and hot.

"You must understand, David," Seref said. "I don't make any money on this boat. I take nothing. When it is all finished, you give me some commission, what you think is right. But I don't take any money now. All is for the boat."

I listened to this and knew it was crap. He was getting a commission every time I bought a nail or a piece of wood.

"I don't make any money on this boat," he said. "I build it like it is my boat. I try to do everything right."

"I appreciate your efforts," I said. "But the deck caulking should last at least twenty years. This deck caulking lasted about a week. So it has to be replaced. And I'm not going to pay. I already paid for caulking the deck."

"David, really you push too much. I cannot do this. Where do I get the money for this?"

"I don't care," I said. "Just do it."

We walked on without speaking for a while, then Seref said, "You do not know me."

I didn't respond. I actually liked Seref, and this was difficult for me. I didn't like to push, but I had to answer to my lenders. It didn't make sense to pay for the deck twice on a new boat. Seref was going to have to fix it.

Talvi, the poet who would be teaching the writing workshop during this charter, arrived in the evening, followed by Steve, a friend I had invited on the trip for free. As long as the trips were nearly empty and still had to be run, I could easily invite a friend.

The two of them were thrilled to be in Turkey. They had dinner with Nancy while I kept working on the boat.

In the morning, we had just enough time to clean up from the construction projects, unload all of the workmen and their tools, and finish provisioning. We had only two paying guests: a friend of mine named Cristal and her friend Jen. Both were getting discounts, so there were no guests paying full fare.

Just before we left, I called Amber in California. I was pulling in some new loans despite everything, but I wasn't keeping up with my bills. The loans were only $10,000 to

$20,000 at a time now. It was a week into August, and so far I had accumulated about $450,000 in private loans, far more than I had thought I would need for the entire project. That didn't count the $125,000 I owed on just my one Stanford American Express card, which would soon shut down because even with a 120-day grace period and juggling my three other Amex cards, I wouldn't be able to pay enough of the balance.

I had to survive until the middle of October, two months away, for John's loan. On my last round of bill-paying the week before, I'd had long phone conversations with Amex reps, explaining the situation regarding the balance on my Stanford Amex card. I was running trips for Stanford Continuing Studies, and yes, I would be able to repay the amounts, but no, I didn't have the funds yet. I was running this whole travel program, and I needed to have the cash to keep the trips going. What I told them was true, but I also didn't emphasize that I was on my own in this business—that if things went bad, Stanford wasn't going to bail me out. These were my own losses I was taking, not Stanford's.

In addition to being behind on Amex bills and behind on money for construction, I was also running short on cash for operating the charters. I needed more diesel, but I didn't have the money. I would probably run out before the end of this charter, so I needed to come up with a solution soon.

We motored into the bay and anchored at Cleopatra's Baths. It was sunny and bright, pine trees reaching down to where ruins lay submerged in about ten feet of water. We snorkeled and swam around the ruins. I enjoyed it but felt preoccupied.

I found some solace hanging out with my friend Steve. He played harmonica and had interesting tales from his few days in Turkey. He had been told by a taxi driver, for instance, that the current tomato glut was Monica Lewinsky's fault. "I know, I know," he said. "It sounds strange. But here's how it works." He was doing these exaggerated gestures with his hands, cutting them up and down through the air, clearing the way for a story, holding his harmonica in one hand. It was late in the day, before dinner, and we had the forward deck to ourselves. "Clinton's embarrassed about the whole Monica Lewinsky thing, so to divert attention, he flies to Kosovo. This makes Americans think more about Kosovo, so they decide not to travel to places like Turkey, so no one is eating in the tourist restaurants, and the restaurants stop buying tomatoes. So now there's a giant tomato glut and the price has fallen and farmers are going out of business. It's all Monica's fault."

I also found solace with Nancy. We went kayaking in the evenings.

"I could ask my dad," she said. "He might give you a loan."

"No," I said. "It would be better to avoid that, don't you think?"

"I'll just ask," she said. "It can't hurt."

I thought it was a terrible idea, but I didn't say no again. I was that desperate. I had to at least consider any possibility.

Our next stop was Fethiye, where we toured local ruins. We climbed two hundred stone steps to a Lycian cliff tomb overlooking the harbor, and as we stood in the shade of this ancient monument, our guide told us that Alexander the Great had wanted to take this town but couldn't. Something about the narrow harbor or the prowess of the local militia. So one of Alexander's generals, Amyntas, sent a bunch of soldiers into town disguised as musicians, their weapons hidden in their instruments. Once inside, the soldiers played a memorable little ditty and opened the city to Alexander, who left Amyntas behind to govern.

I liked these tales. It was always hard to know how much was truth and how much was local myth, fabricated over time, like the stories Seref was telling me, but they were certainly entertaining.

We drove in a minivan through town and then along a highway through a great valley, chatting and enjoying the landscape. We crossed into another valley and climbed, finally, into foothills and stopped at Tlos, which became my favorite site that summer.

Tlos sits on a rocky bluff rising from the Xanthos Valley. It has Lycian tombs carved on its lower faces, including one with Bellerophon riding Pegasus, probably a tomb for royalty, some of whom claimed descent from Bellerophon. Above these are house tombs cut deep into the rock and a few sarcophagi standing on the more level area. The acropolis at the top of the bluff is mostly Ottoman, from as late as the nineteenth century. The view from here is idyllic. High mountains behind, snowcapped even in summer, forested foothills, and a broad, fertile valley leading to the sea, holding the ruins of Xanthos, Patara, and Letoon. Truly one of the most beautiful places any of us had ever seen.

Behind the bluff that contains the tombs is a great field, now growing corn, which was once the agora, or marketplace. There are still a lot of significant structures scattered up the hill, including a large stadium, aqueducts, and our favorite, the baths. We had seen a lot of Roman baths, but these were on a cliff overlooking the valley, the arches still intact; we could sit under them and gaze out on much the same view the ancients enjoyed, with the same warm breezes coming up from the valley.

While we took these tours, my Turkish crew was working hard on the varnish and other tasks, doing a great job. I wasn't making any progress with the deck seams, however. And in Kas, farther down the coast, I ran into some new difficulties.

Kas is a charming little town. The harbor area has narrow cobblestone lanes closed to vehicle traffic. Up a hill is a large Lycian sarcophagus right in the middle of the street. The shops cater mostly to tourists but are small enough to be cute.

I needed to renew my tourist visa, so while my guests enjoyed the town on the morning of our arrival, I went to the ferry, planning to hop over to the Greek island that was only a few miles away. The round-trip, including paperwork, would take about two hours. But after I had bought my ticket and boarded, I was called off the ferry because my personal visa was linked to my boat. I couldn't be cleared out of the country unless my boat was also cleared out.

I had discussed this issue explicitly with Seref when he was doing my charter paperwork in Bodrum. It was supposed to have been arranged so I wasn't chained to the boat. I had paid for various licenses and permits and had even paid a $6,000 bed tax for running charters: it had been expensive, and I had expected it to be done right.

I called Seref, who told me there was nothing he could do. I would have to take the boat with me to the Greek island and back.

"But what about my guests?" I asked him. "And it's Saturday. What if I can't clear out today?"

"I am sorry, David. But Kas is good place. Your guests will like. And Saturday is no problem."

So I collected my boat papers to clear out of customs and immigration. Then I'd clear in and out of Greece and back into Turkey.

When I found the customs office, though, it was locked. The hours posted on the door showed that they should have been open, but they weren't.

I asked in the restaurant next door if they knew when the customs officers would be back.

"He's never there," a pretty young woman told me. Then her parents, apparently the owners of the restaurant, told me the customs inspector always took time off for his own business and let people wait here for days. He was not responsible, they said, and I should report his absence to the police station.

I didn't want to become involved in local politics, but hours later, after I had called the number posted on the door and asked around and was still waiting, I finally went to the police, with Muhsin as a translator. I found the port authority section and asked if they could just clear me out.

My request was too complicated for the guys at the front desk, so I was ushered into the office of an inspector who said he'd be happy to help. I would only have to fill out a statement saying I had been unable to find the customs inspector. Then he could clear me.

So I filled out the statement and waited. The clearance didn't come, so I asked again, through Muhsin, and was told that I would still need the customs inspector. And he wouldn't be in on Sunday, so I would have to wait until Monday morning.

"But I just filled out the statement so that I wouldn't need to see him," I said.

"I'm sorry, but you must come back Monday morning," the police inspector told me in English. "And we keep your passports. We give back to you on Monday."

I managed to remain calm, because I couldn't afford trouble with the police, but really this was a bit unbelievable. Muhsin tried talking with the inspector again, as politely as possible, to discover other options, but there didn't seem to be any.

Everyone was annoyed by the delay, but especially Cristal's friend Jen. She was upset to be trapped somewhere on her vacation. A few hours before, the town had seemed lovely. Now it was a prison. I arranged for a tour to Saklikent, which would fill the entire next day, but we were spending too much time parked in one port. We were supposed to keep moving and seeing new places.

Saklikent is a deep canyon near Tlos, a narrow gap in the face of steep mountains lining the eastern side of the Xanthos valley. The river is cold and silty, rushing out of the canyon to twist along gravel spits to the ocean. Restaurants line either side where it pours out, with platforms for tables built over the water. Fifty feet up from the restaurants, at the entrance of the canyon, a walkway built along the rock wall leads to another restaurant tucked inside. From here, the water was low enough to cross at the fork of the river's two sources, just inside the canyon walls, and hike up the drier source, the most spectacular part of the canyon. The walls were marble, polished by the river in winter. As we continued up, we passed beneath natural cathedrals, the marble colored red and pink and even a bluish tint.

As in all of Turkey, no safety measures had been taken. Every time I walked that canyon, rocks came down to shatter against nearby stone or splash into the water, and we all ducked, too late, then grinned sheepishly at one another.

After hiking the canyon, we sat on cushions in one of the restaurants, the water rushing beneath, and ordered Turkish bread that was fried and filled with honey or cheese. Then I rented inner tubes for everyone, along with a guide, and we waded into the ice-cold water under an extremely hot sun, perfect conditions for tubing. Real squeals as we hit standing waves and took frigid water down our backs or fronts, but also enough heat from the sun to warm us back up.

I loved the view, the mountains a spinning panorama. It was a great outing, diminished only by the fact of returning to Kas and knowing we weren't leaving the next day until I had cleared out, in, out, and in.

By 7:30 A.M., I was waiting at the door of the customs office, but again it was deserted. I tried calling and asking around, but no luck. The customs inspector finally showed up about 10:30. I went in and politely asked for a clearance, showing him my papers, but he had already heard about the weekend's events.

"You file a complaint against me," he said. "Why you do this?"

"I didn't mean to file a complaint," I said. "I thought I was filling out paperwork to get a clearance from the police."

"Ah," he said. He was smoking, as all Turks do, especially in closed spaces. He was a young, handsome man, obviously taken with himself as an inspector and insulted by my complaint. "So you make a mistake?"

"Yes," I said.

"Yes, yes, you certainly make a mistake," he said. "You make a mistake with me." He smoked some more and looked at the various walls with nothing on them. Behind him was a large portrait of Ataturk, which seemed to be the only portrait of anyone hanging in any office in Turkey. Modern Turkey was basically his idea, so this was appropriate. "You go to the police and take back this complaint, then you come see me again."

"Okay," I said. "I'm sorry." There was no point in fighting. This man had the power to keep me in port for months if he felt like it.

I went to the police station and retracted my complaint. Curiously, they weren't disappointed to lose it. The other day they had expressed annoyance with the customs inspector, but now they talked of him as their great friend and colleague. I had clearly been made a pawn in some kind of local power struggle. My side had lost, and now no one else was on my side.

They sent me and my passport back to the customs inspector under police escort, as if I couldn't be trusted not to attempt escape.

Then the customs inspector called in the immigration inspector, and they discussed at length the various difficulties of my noxious passport. When they finally stamped it, they charged me over $100 for a clearance, which is supposed to be free. Then they lectured me a bit, blew smoke in my face, and sent me back to the police. The police made me wait for a while, then finally cleared me and charged another $40 just for fun.

It was almost 1 P.M. before I was back on board. I cast off with only Muhsin as crew, since Ercan and Baresh didn't have the required visas, and we motored for about half an hour to cross the channel.

The harbor on this Greek island was picturesque and completely different from Kas, the architecture and layout and feel of the town much more European. There was more money here, and greater order, and a general sense of drowsiness. No one moving very quickly.

The Greek customs officer, in his middle years, was sitting outside his office, on a chair against the wall. "You are English?" he asked.

"No," I said. "Just the flag. I'm American."

"And you?" he asked Muhsin. "Turkish?"

"Yes," Muhsin nodded.

The customs officer made some sour faces, letting us know how he felt about Americans and Turks. His lips pinched closed but his tongue moved around in his mouth, wanting to break free. This was 1999. The Greeks were supporters of the Kurdistan Workers' Party and Ocalan and resented U.S. and Israeli cooperation with the Turkish government in his capture. They were Christian, but not nearly as closely allied to the United States as Muslim Turkey. And they had Cypress and all the coastal islands as sore spots with the Turks. Just a few years before, the two countries had almost gone to war over possession of a few small, uninhabited pieces of rock sticking up along the coast. So this customs officer was ruminating a bit, and he was making us ruminate, too. But finally he stood up, walked into his office, and gave us our entry and clearance.

It was 3 P.M. by the time we were docked again in Kas, and I still had to clear back into Turkey before we could move on to the next port.

I went to the customs inspector first. He was in his office, which was convenient, and unusual, but he also had made up some new regulations for me. He said my charter paperwork from Bodrum was incorrect and I would have to obtain a doctor's clearance and pay a lighthouse tax. "Maybe in Bodrum they do not know these regulations," he said, smoking and gazing absentmindedly at his blank walls. "But here we are very careful."

I knew he was full of shit, but knowledge is not power when it comes to dealing with government officials, so I had to run to the police, then to the other side of town to find the doctor, then to a notary, then back to the doctor, then to the police, and finally to customs and immigration. By the end, I had paid more than $500 just to clear in, almost all of which was bogus. I left Kas in a foul mood. And my guests weren't happy, either; it was after six by the time we left. We arrived at our next port long after dark.

The rest of the trip went well. It's hard to beat the ruins and coves and towns along that coast, and it's hard to beat a poetry workshop with Talvi Ansel. The only difficulties were when Ercan hit on Steve, by blowing in his ear, and my lack of money. When it was time to get diesel, though, Steve helped me out. He loaned me $2,200, which would fill our tanks almost halfway.

We did have one other problem that trip, which was that the air conditioners leaked water under the beds from condensation, and this water made the cheap wood-laminate flooring buckle. So I told Seref, and he promised me he would have the air-conditioning man fix the drains to the units, and he would do something about the flooring. He was vague about what and when, of course.

Then a huge earthquake hit near Istanbul. Oddly, this was one event that summer in Turkey that had no effect on my business. Although the quake was an enormous national tragedy, killing eighteen thousand people and leaving hundreds of thousands homeless, it left the airport in Istanbul strangely intact. Which shows, despite other indications to the contrary, that perhaps luck is only luck.

MY NEXT CHARTER was a course on Homer's *Odyssey* taught by Charlie Junkerman, who was my boss at Stanford, and Rush Rehm, his friend in the classics department. Four adult students had signed up, which was a record for paying guests that summer. Everyone arrived in high spirits, charmed by the medieval walls of Antalya's harbor and excited to sail the coast that Homer and Odysseus had sailed.

On this trip, we had the usual Turkish guides for the ruins but we also had Rush, who was extremely knowledgeable and likeable. In Myra, as we gazed at tombs carved into the cliffs, he told us the stories of the figures depicted. As we toured the large and well-preserved Roman theater, he told us about theater conventions of the time. The group had read quite a bit of background material about the sites we were visiting, and the debates were lively. This was what I had hoped for in setting up these educational charters. Vacations that were explorations and adventures, not just lying in the sun and drinking.

Rush and Charlie held class on the aft deck every morning,

the students in their swimsuits and snacking on olives. It was perfect, and if it hadn't been for the war in Kosovo, it might have been a viable business.

Each charter, we toured the ruins of Phaselis, Olympos, the Church of St. Nicholas, Myra, Kekova and Kekova Island, Patara, Letoon, Xanthos, Tlos, Fethiye, and Cleopatra's baths, in addition to hiking and tubing at Saklikent and exploring lovely seaside towns and coves from Antalya to Gocek. It was hard, after setting all of this up and seeing how wonderful the trips could be, to know that the business was failing.

I continued to have problems with the boat, too. In Kas, I woke in the morning to Ercan and Muhsin knocking at my door.

"There is a problem," Muhsin said. "You need to see."

They led me onto the deck, then forward to the port bow and asked me to look over the side.

I hesitated for a moment, wondering what good fortune this town had brought me now. When I bent over and looked down at the waterline, I could see a piece of the paint hanging loose. This was difficult to believe. The paint and the thick epoxy beneath it are supposed to stick to the hull, of course. The paint job had taken months.

I called Seref on Ercan's cell phone, up on the bow, away from my guests. Charlie and Rush had gotten up early, though, and they knew. Charlie gave me a look of pity. I think he understood all the troubles I had gone through to try to make these charters happen.

"The paint's falling off the hull," I told Seref, who went through his usual expressions of disbelief: how can this be true, this can't happen, this isn't possible, etc. "It's true," I said. "I'm looking at a large piece of paint and epoxy just hanging at the waterline. And I need to move the boat now, to sail to the next port, which means some of the paint is about to be stripped off of the boat. You have to fix this."

"But how? How can this be?"

"I don't know," I said. "But we might have to sail to

Bodrum after this charter and haul out for an emergency paint job, maybe ten days. You'll have to rent another boat to run the next charter, which has only four people, and then, after the painting, we'll motor the 220 miles again from Bodrum to Antalya to pick up the last charter. I can't think of anything else. I shouldn't have to be dealing with this. When you build a boat, you should build it to last more than a couple of weeks. You're going to redo the deck, too, and take out that laminate crap on the floors in the staterooms. It's all buckled now, so that some of the doors don't even close. Please arrange all of this today."

I tried to tell my guests in light, funny tones that our paint was falling off, as if it were somehow amusing, and then we pulled out of the harbor and headed up the coast.

It was a lovely day, with calm water and blue skies, and all of us, guests and crew, took turns leaning over the side to watch large patches of white paint and paste flex and shiver, then fall off, sometimes in sections as big as four or five feet long by three feet high. It was all coming off, one whole side of the boat. There was nothing I could do but keep to the schedule and come to grips with the fact that we now looked like a military vessel, stripped down to our gray primer over steel, all the welding ribs showing. I felt terrible about polluting the water, but it just wasn't realistic to try to recover each of the fifty pieces as they ripped off, especially since they sank quickly. And I couldn't have just stayed in Kas. That's the main rule in charter. Unless you're held hostage by terrorists or government authorities, you stick to the itinerary and give the guests their vacation, no matter what's happening to the boat or the crew.

The rest of that charter, I was making arrangements. By the time we arrived in Gocek, there was another, smaller charter boat waiting at the dock for my next guests. Seref and I had fought over who would pay for this, and I had lost. He would pay for the emergency haul in Bodrum, and the labor to recaulk the deck. He would also redo the floors, and repaint the boat, but the paint company would have to pay for the new paint, and I would have to pay for the difference in cost between the two kinds of deck caulking, the new wood for the floors, and the smaller charter boat for my guests.

Out of the water, the boat looked like a yacht on one side and a battleship on the other. Seref's cousin and Mustafa, the owner of the yard that had built my hull, came down to look at it, Seref's cousin rich as ever, a handsome, tall, European-looking man with possible mafia connections who wore thousands of dollars of the finest clothing. Mustafa, shorter and homely, smoking his pipe as always. Then the insurance man arrived, then the representative from the paint company, and everyone examined my boat before driving to Mustafa's yard to look at a boat under construction. The hull had been fared with epoxy paste, and small circles were drawn all over its surface to show bubbles forming under the paste, sections that were pulling away from the hull. Seref's cousin's new boat, painted with the same batch of paint, had already been launched. As with my boat, large strips of its paint had fallen off. Finally we gathered in Mustafa's office to discuss the problem.

This discussion took some time. In the end, we agreed the company would provide two coats of quick-drying epoxy, two topcoats, and two coats of bottom paint. The meeting had been frustrating and long, but now we could move forward quickly.

This turned out not to be the case, however. I had to leave for a day and a half to meet my charter guests and their professor down the coast, and when I returned, I was disappointed. I told Seref we weren't going to make it at this pace, but he ignored me until it was too late. Probably this was intentional. He forced me into a compromise. The floors in the staterooms would not be done until the end of September, just before I sailed for Mexico.

Seref and I were not getting along. I told him directly, as we stood in the hot sun in the dust: "You promise things, but then you don't deliver. You're too slow. You should have had ten guys working on this immediately, but you didn't listen to me, and now you're not going to be able to do it on time. Which means, to me, that you're doing this on purpose, because I know you're a smart man."

"David, we will do this job. Really, you must not talk like this."

"How are you going to do it, Seref? You're already too late."

These conversations usually ended in silence, filled with what I believed to be mutual regret. Too many things had gone wrong, the boat an enormous weight dragging both of us down. We took turns making excuses. Seref made excuses about botched and late construction; I made excuses about late payments. The war in Kosovo was killing both of our businesses. He was doing less than 40 percent of his usual business, even with the Brits, who tend not to be deterred much by war or terrorism, and he was suffering especially from his new rental cars. I suspected he had bought some of these cars in the winter using my money. I suspected that a month or two of construction in the winter had not actually happened. But I couldn't know for sure, and there was no possibility of recourse in the Turkish courts, anyway.

I spent every day at the boat, trying to hurry the job along. I also tried to encourage the use of safety harnesses, since the men with the sanders were up on scaffolding. They laughed at me, the silly American trying to hand out his safety equipment, but one day, after I made Baresh and Ercan put on sailing harnesses with tethers leading up to stanchions, Baresh slipped and fell off the scaffolding. His sander and the board he was standing on fell twenty feet to the ground, but he was left dangling in the air, held by his tether. Several men pulled him up on deck, and after that I was teased less. Ercan, however, blamed the fall on the harness and tether. "If he not have this equipment, he never fall."

I'd had other impossible arguments with Ercan that summer. On one of the earlier charters, for instance, I had asked him to install siphon breaks for the bilge pump discharges, but he refused. "This not my job," he said. "This things not necessary. This not my job."

I didn't like arguing with him, so instead I tried to show him. We had some water in the bilge, so I had him watch the water level as I turned the pump on and off. Each time I turned it on, the water level went down. Each time I turned it off, the water level went up and kept rising until I turned it on again. "You see?" I asked. "The discharge has formed a siphon. This is what happened to the engines, too. The water coming in from the bilge pump could actually sink us. Which is why we have to use either a one-way valve or a siphon break."

Ercan smiled. "It doesn't do this before."

"That's because we just filled our water tank and partially filled diesel," I said. "It will happen every time we're heavy. Ecrem should have cut the discharge holes higher, but he didn't."

"Other boats don't need this," Ercan said. "I see many other boats. This is not necessary."

I lost it at this point. I had just showed him clearly, beyond any doubt, how it could sink the boat. "You'll sink," I said. "Someday, on some other Turkish piece of shit, you'll sink. I promise you. And it will be exactly what you deserve."

In fact, the day after Baresh slipped and was saved by his harness, Seref was called away suddenly because his own boat was sinking, right in Bodrum harbor. This was the boat he had admonished me with one day when I insulted his construction prowess, the first real sailboat in Bodrum. He was cagey about it afterward, and he never did tell me exactly what happened, but he admitted that the boat sank from siphoning. By that point in the summer I had lost all respect for Seref or anyone I had met in Turkey as sailors or engineers or honest businessmen. I know that sounds uncharitable, but I base it solely on the facts of my experience. I had not arrived with a bad attitude. If anything, I was their dream of a naive and trusting American. I trusted them and managed to convince seventeen private lenders to trust them. I had been an enormous fool, and now it was too late.

By day we worked on the hull, by night on the deck. Seref wouldn't hire enough men to do both jobs at once. I refused to pay more for the job, and I didn't have the money anyway, and I couldn't figure out how to force Seref to do more than he was doing. I was already withholding the last money that was due. I had already threatened an end to future business. I had tried to shame him. And of course I had asked nicely. I didn't know what else to do.

The hull and deck were grueling jobs. Some of the epoxy on the hull was holding, which made grinding difficult. The two coats of faring we applied were thin, not hiding the weld ribs, and we had to use a less glossy top paint to hide the flaws.

The deck seams were cleaned out inch by inch with small tools, then caulked with an air-powered gun, Ercan and his brother and I taking turns late into the night, the black caulking getting all over us. I was frantic to finish and get back in the water for the next charter.

When we did finally launch, the paint job wasn't quite done. We motored around to Bodrum, and the painter put on the last coat right there in the middle of the harbor, using my dinghy, which became completely spattered with white paint. The job looked like crap, far inferior to the original paint. I would need a new paint job as soon as I could afford it. Until then the boat would look like a ferry or a tug rather than a yacht.

We set off that evening for Antalya, hoping to arrive the next day before dark. We still didn't have a compass, and the crew were frustrated and spun in circles occasionally, but we did make it.

THE MORNING WAS hectic with provisioning and cleaning, then the guests arrived. I was happy to see Rand and Lee, two of my lenders. Rand had sailed with me in the British Virgin Islands and the Sea of Cortez and had been the one to originally encourage me to get a bigger boat. Lee, his wife, was a vice president at Sun Microsystems. After this twelve-day charter, they would be staying for the trip through the Med to Gibraltar and the Canary Islands. Another lender, Elizabeth, the former wife of a bigwig CEO, had invited half a dozen of her friends, so no one on this charter was a paying guest. It wasn't just the war in Kosovo that was killing my business. I had also been too generous with the terms of the loans, offering free charter as well as principal and interest. I should have made the lenders pay at least the expenses of a charter, including diesel, crew, slip fees, customs fees, and food. Instead I was picking up the tab. Further proof of my foolishness. Self-reflection was becoming an increasingly unpleasant activity.

I spent as much of this trip as possible with Rand and Lee

and Nancy. We strolled the ancient marble streets of cities such as Phaselis, with its lovely coves on either side, a city that had attracted Alexander, Rhodes pirates, and whoever else was big at any particular time. And one afternoon—in Kas, of all places—as we sat outside a small café and had ice cream, Rand and Lee expressed interest in becoming something more like partners in the boat. Lee was retiring in a year or so, and they loved the boat and the trips I ran, and they also could see the financial strain I was under, so they wanted to help out.

This came as a tremendous relief. Amex had shut down all four cards. They wanted everything paid in full. I was out of cash and at the end of other credit, and I would have expenses for the crossing to Mexico.

By the end of the charter, Rand and Lee, though they had already loaned me $100,000 in various stages, agreed to lend $150,000 more, interest-free. I remember whispering about it at night in bed with Nancy. Rand and Lee were in the next stateroom, so I had to be quiet. But I was so excited. I was going to make it. Everything was going to work out. With this loan and then John's loan I could clear all the cards, make my first interest payments in December to the lenders, and have enough cash to get through the winter in Mexico. Then I would need to have some better charter seasons, of course. But I felt like a free man again.

The more I thought about this new loan the more stunned I was by the generosity of it. Rand and Lee were loaning me a total of $250,000, most of it without interest, and they were even giving me ten years to repay the principal, instead of the usual three. This was the time of "angel" investors in Silicon Valley, but those angels usually tried to take most of the equity of any company they invested in. Rand and Lee were not taking any equity at all. They were the real thing.

Rand and Lee left on a four-day tour by car as Nancy and the crew and I motored back to Bodrum. We'd have a few days to take on diesel and provisions and do last-minute work on the boat before sailing for Mexico. And we'd be switching from the Turkish crew to an American crew, to avoid hassles with customs and immigration in various countries.

These days were busy but also much easier than the rest of the summer, because the financial crush had been lifted. Amber was happy to hear about the money coming in, after having to juggle bills all summer, and reassured me that she had just spoken with John, whose loan would arrive in about three weeks.

Not everything went smoothly, though. Now that the new seams had cured, Ercan and another man were sanding the entire deck with a large grinder, and naturally Ercan was barefoot. I had told him to wear boots many times that summer, but he was always scoffing at my safety worries, and this time the grinder caught a bit of deck, jumped, and tore up his foot and hand pretty badly. It didn't saw through, but it mangled skin and several toes and cut the bone.

We rushed him to the hospital, which was already a familiar place. A few weeks earlier, Seref's son had been run over by a car while riding his bicycle through one of Bodrum's narrow streets. He pulled through without permanent damage, and Ercan was going to do the same, but I couldn't help thinking how easy it was to die or lose a limb here, how cheap life was.

I stayed with Ercan through that first afternoon and evening, and I paid for all his care. I also gave him extra cash in addition to his pay. There's no workers' health insurance to speak of in Turkey. Employers just pay if an employee gets hurt, or else the employee is out of luck. The cost of medical care, fortunately, is about a tenth of what it is in the United States.

As we came to our last day in Bodrum, Seref was holding all of my papers. Ostensibly this was because he was clearing customs and immigration for me. But it was also a power play. I had to pay him the last two or three thousand I owed before I could go. I promised I would make the payment within a week, with a transfer from the States, since I didn't have the cash now, and he finally agreed to this, seeing no other option, but then he wanted to go for a little walk to discuss his "commission."

The boat that was supposed to cost $300,000 or $350,000 and be perfect had in fact cost $600,000 and was full of flaws I would be fixing for years, but Seref expected a bonus for all of the good work he had done. He wanted his tip to be based on the total cost, including the original purchase of the hull and the cost of the items I had shipped. He wanted 15 percent, which was $90,000. I knew that he had been collecting commissions all along and had probably bought some of his new rental car fleet with my money during the winter, delaying the construction. But for now I had to pretend a commission was coming so he would let me leave.

Seref had one hand on the back of my neck as we walked along. It was evening, very balmy, the Bodrum waterfront a place I was actually quite fond of and was going to miss, even the mopeds sputtering past.

"I build this boat for you like it is my own boat," he said. "Do you like your boat?"

"Yes," I said. "It's beautiful. Thank you. And though we've had some bad moments, I want you to know how much I appreciate the work you've done for me."

He seemed to relax a bit. "You are my friend," he said. "Most men demand full commission before the boat leaves, but I know your money, that you have no money until you get this loan from John, and your schedule, and I know you won't forget me when you leave here."

"No," I said. "I'll send the commission as soon as I get the loan from John. And you'll have to come visit this winter in Mexico, and then I'll be back here next summer. We have the new thing for the Brits next summer, after all."

"Yes," he said. He had made a new alliance in the past few weeks with a British travel company that catered to older guests. He had told them about my educational charters and they seemed interested. The next summer, using leased boats, we were going to run educational charters for hundreds of British senior citizens, and I was going to supply all of the professors and set up the curriculum.

I didn't believe any of this, of course. It was just a ploy by Seref to encourage me to pay his commission.

"Yes," Seref said again. "This will be very good business for us." Then he stopped, and I stopped, too, since he still had his big hand on my neck. He reached into his pocket with his other hand and pulled out an old compass. "I have a gift for you. My father give me this compass, for my first boat."

"Seref," I said. "I can't take that. That has so many memories for you."

"Please," he said. "My friend."

So I took the compass and made a great show of my gratitude and how much his friendship meant to me and how much I was going to miss him.

"Come," he said, satisfied finally, or at least realizing this was the best he was going to get. "We go to my office for the papers."

We picked up the papers, including passports and the registration for the boat, then I was back on board, the boat and new crew and guests ready, and I was greatly relieved. I was going to get out of here in one piece. It was dark, about 10 P.M., our spreader lights on as we pulled anchor and freed our lines. Baresh was waving goodbye to us. He was a sweet young man. He had been paid the least, and I had given him the biggest tip, which I was glad of now.

We motored out from under the magnificent castle, set our sails, and escaped across the wine-dark sea.

Part Two

MALTA AT SUNRISE is one of the more spectacular things a sailor can see. It's always a pleasure to view an island for the first time from the water, to approach it as the ancients did, as travelers did through all the ages until the airplane. But Malta is a special treat, because at first you see only lovely hills, light beige and pink in the light before the sun has risen fully, with what seem to be cliff faces, and it is only as you come closer that you see that some of this rock, some of these cliffs, are in fact fortifications and monuments, built from the stone of the island. You begin to make out the medieval walls and the towers. You watch the city make itself in the light, and still you don't see anything modern, but only what a medieval traveler would have seen. And this impression remains mostly intact, even as you draw close. Only after you're inside the harbor do you notice the smaller shops and buses and cars and power lines. Malta is an enchanted island, the place I was most eager to visit of all our ports from Turkey to Mexico.

I radioed for a slip and was assigned an agent, who would

take care of our other needs as well. I had quite a few things to buy and fix while in Malta. One of the inverters had blown out, and we needed a spotlight, a pump, several spare parts, and some hardware. This in addition to filling diesel, propane, water, and provisioning for the next leg to Ibiza, in the Spanish Balearic Islands.

I was afraid, with all of this to do, that I wouldn't see Malta at all, and this in fact is what happened. While my guests and Nancy and even the crew were able to tour the island, I worked nonstop. I heard about the Blue Grotto and other places I had wanted to visit, but I didn't see them. A lot of pirate movies have been filmed on Malta, because of the spectacular coastline, and renting these movies was going to be the closest I would get.

The only taste of Malta available to me was the language. Because Malta is a small island country in the middle of the Mediterranean and has been an important trading port for thousands of years, its language is a blend of the tongues of all the sailors and conquerors who have passed through. When I first heard Maltese, I actually laughed, because I thought someone was just being very funny. But it was no joke. The blend is mostly Arabic and Sicilian but includes Greek, Spanish, French, English, and other tongues, including African tongues, with a bit of the Swedish chef thrown in. It's the most improbable, liquid, gorgeous mess of language I have ever heard.

This humored me as I went about my tasks. But I was preoccupied by the fact that business at home in California was not good. Amber was not selling our winter trips in Mexico.

There was no reason these trips should not have sold. I had a famous professor teaching the archaeology of the Maya, an excellent Spanish language instructor, a famous poet, and other solid offerings. Mine was the only overnight charter boat on that entire coast south of Cancún. And Cancún was an easy place to fly into. I had advertising through the University of San Diego as well as through Stanford. The advertising budget was a bit short for magazine ads and direct-mail post-cards, but the numbers were still far too low. Amber just wasn't good at selling trips, or she wasn't trying.

I was also worried that she wasn't paying bills correctly. I sent an e-mail with precise instructions for the new loan from Rand and Lee; exact amounts were to be paid on each of my dozen credit cards. I was so late on so many bills that I had to be careful what I paid when, to keep all of the various creditors sufficiently appeased.

We finished our preparations and set sail for Ibiza. My crew were college students taking fall semester off. Nick, Charlie Junkerman's son, had suffered up the California coast with me two summers earlier, on the way to my first charter season in the San Juans with *Grendel*. I had promised him and his parents that this trip would be better, an enjoyable cruise through the Med and then an easy downwind sail across the Atlantic and Caribbean to the Yucatán. Emi had been a student in one of my undergraduate courses. She was from Homer, Alaska, and had spent many seasons working on her family's commercial fishing boat. Her boyfriend, Matt, also an Alaskan commercial fisherman, had joined us even though I wasn't paying him.

The trip through the Strait of Sicily was rough. So when we pulled into Ibiza after three days at sea, I was tired. A lovely harbor, with a huge castle on the point, but it was an overcast, blustery day. As I entered the narrow fairway to the marina, the wind was gusting at over thirty knots from behind, which made our entire boat act like a sail. I had the engines in reverse as I was blown down the fairway past dozens of multimillion-dollar motor yachts.

I saw very little of Ibiza. It's one of the most famous party towns in the world, with clubs that pound all night. We were seeing it in mid-October, though, after the high season, so it was quieter. The castle was magnificent and much better preserved and more accessible than any other I had visited in the Mediterranean. I felt the full enchantment of the place at night with Nancy, walking the fortified walls lit in green and white, following mazes down inside the castle, stone passageways that twisted and turned and finally emerged in some new vista of lights overlooking the harbor and city. I longed to have just a little more time, but I was on a schedule, meeting people in Gibraltar, the Canaries, and St. Lucia, and I had to keep the boat running. I had to arrive in Mexico on time for my new permits and licenses and other preparations for the winter charters.

So we sailed for Gibraltar, Nancy and the crew and I. No guests. And we hit no weather at all. It was flat calm. Reflective, like a mountain lake, with no boats and no wind. Even when I had hit a huge calm in the Pacific a thousand miles out from Hawaii on *Grendel* and seen a blue whale, I had been able to detect a very gradual swell, but on this trip there was no swell at all. We motored without sails across endless glass, laughing with each other at the oddity of it. Our last night, we passed through an extensive fishing fleet, lights everywhere on the water, like fireflies. Off in the distance were two lighter patches of sky that over the hours became the two Pillars of Hercules, Gibraltar and Europe on the right, Morocco and Africa on the left. Two such different worlds so close to touching. We could see the lights of individual buildings on both shores, and heavy shipping traffic in between. Scores of tankers and freighters were anchored in the shallows, our radar dotted up for miles.

We entered the Bay of Gibraltar, passing just southwest of the famous rock, which was lit by spotlights, and waited half an hour or so for daylight to make our approach into a marina. I felt lucky to be experiencing all of this, voyaging from one end of the Mediterranean to the other, and I think the crew felt the same way. In the future, though, I wanted to have the luxury of visiting every port. We had passed so close to Tunis, an African port, but the schedule hadn't allowed a stop. We had passed

Sicily, also, without stopping. We had sailed close enough to see these places, the outline of their mountains, had studied them through the binoculars, knowing we were missing everything. I missed Turkey already like a second home, ached for it despite all the hassles. And what about these other countries, if only I could spend some time in them?

In Gib, as the locals refer to it, we were joined by Barbara, one of my lenders who had already been on trips in the San Juan Islands, the British Virgin Islands, and Mexico. She was happy to be on vacation, away from the responsibilities of her law firm and kids, and she was anxious to head out.

My three crew were busy roaming Gibraltar for various spares and offshore equipment. The entire country is only three miles long and a mile wide, a warren of small shops that seem nearly invisible but are known, without exception, by every Gibraltarian. And the landmarks are houses and neighborhoods, rather than streets. "That's near Imossi House, just before Irish Town," they'll say. Gates and walls are also used as landmarks. The walls run everywhere, large stone structures with various important gates commemorating war. The whole country is a small wart on Spain's backside (which Spain would like to have removed), but it looks nothing like Spain, and it even has its own weather, because of the Rock, which catches what is usually the only cloud for hundreds of miles and then manages to squeeze some rain and cold out of it, while Spain remains sunny and hot.

The main chandlery in Gibraltar is Sheppards, very near our marina. They can boast the highest prices for marine hardware anywhere in the world, combined with the very worst customer service. They can offer all this because they have no competition, a condition guaranteed to continue into perpetuity because of tight, nepotistic control over business licenses.

Gibraltar, all in all, is a dark and depressing little place. The bright spots are the pasties and the megayachts. The pasties at Dad's Bakehouse are extremely cheap and tasty: delicious pastry filled with the classic beef, potatoes, carrots, and onion, or variations with chicken or veggies. I was also fond of several fish-and-chips shops. And you can't beat Gibraltar for megayachts. Everyone stops in Gibraltar on their way in or out of the Med, and these largest yachts tend to make their transits every year between the Med and the Caribbean. *Boat International,* the magazine that features them, is the only magazine I treasure, and for each megayacht that pulled up, Nancy and I would pull out the appropriate issue and stroll the dock to gaze at the exterior and check out the interior and specs in the magazine. Megayachts are a ridiculous waste of money, costing $20 million or even ten times more, but they are also among the most beautiful and amazing objects created by humankind. Our favorite was a long blue hull of classic design with a high bow and a narrow stern, a varnished deckhouse and other classic brightwork combined with an ultramodern rig and underbody. The perfect fusion of the traditional and the modern, and as large as three city buses placed end to end.

We made good progress on our work, despite the distraction of these yachts parked right next to us, but the weather turned sour and delayed our departure. It was cold and squally, with a lot of rain and no weather window appearing.

I spent more and more time in the Internet café, fighting Amber. She assured me she had paid bills correctly after we received the $150,000 loan from Rand and Lee. But when I called my various cards to verify, I found she had mispaid my bills by an astounding $48,000. On my biggest Amex card, she had paid $18,000 more than I had asked. This was $18,000 that didn't need to be paid until the next month. She paid over $10,000 on another bill that wasn't yet due. And she didn't pay anything on a $12,000 bill that had to be paid immediately. I couldn't understand how she could be so incompetent.

I had written down the details very clearly and reminded her to double-check when she paid. She was a Stanford graduate, not a complete idiot, so the only explanation was that she didn't care. She had already informed me she was moving on to a new job at the end of the month. A friend of hers had started a dot-com with millions of dollars, so she was getting a job as a product manager, even though she had no idea what that role entailed. And she didn't care if my business went straight into the toilet.

I felt trapped. I should have been in California, saving my business, but I also had to stay with the boat and deliver it to Mexico. The winds were increasing, the weather turning foul, so I couldn't have left the boat even if there had been no deadline for getting to Mexico.

The storm increased to hurricane strength, with winds topping seventy-seven knots on the rock and more than fifty in the harbor. Our huge boat, with almost ten feet of hull from the water to deck level, and then the large pilothouse and thick wooden masts, was exactly broadside to the wind. We used every dock line we had, until there was a web of over twenty lines coming from all our scuppers to every fitting on the dock. We were using winches and cleats and the windlass. But still the wind heeled the boat more than twenty degrees and we had to jump to the dock and back. Most of the time, Barbara couldn't make the leap. Her legs weren't long enough.

On the other side of our concrete finger, megayachts were tied stern-to, their bows facing into the wind, held by double anchors. We watched one of these, a hundred-foot motor-yacht, slip back and grind its stern against the concrete, which bit deep into its fiberglass. My crew and I ran over to help, trying to put fenders between the boat and the dock and yelling over the wind for the yacht's crew. They couldn't hear us, but they could feel and hear the grinding from inside. They came running out, fired up the engines, and put out more fenders, but the forces were enormous.

We had visitors day and night from the dozen or so fifty-foot fiberglass yachts that were downwind of us. If our lines failed, we would, in a matter of seconds, be blown across about fifty feet of water and pulverize all of those little boats, many of which had cost between $300,000 and $600,000. So their owners took a special interest in our lines and how they were secured and whether they would hold. They were of the opinion, of course, that our lines were not thick enough, and they hassled me so continuously I finally went to Sheppards and paid more than $300 for two twenty-five-foot lines. It was a waste of money, but I was under a lot of pressure, from the marina as well as from the boat owners. So in the end we had almost thirty lines holding us to the dock, including two of the thickest that could be purchased in Gibraltar, and though we were heeled over in the wind and bouncing in the waves, we held.

When the winds finally died down, we had been delayed a full week, and another storm was supposed to come soon. A weather window of three or four days, long enough for us to get clear of the area, was predicted, so I decided to make a dash for it.

WE WATCHED THE Pillars of Hercules passing astern on both sides and followed the African shoreline. After an hour or two, we hit large standing waves, almost twenty feet high. We weren't in the mouth of the strait anymore, but even this far out, the tremendous volume of water draining from the Mediterranean to meet Atlantic swells was causing the same kind of standing waves I had seen while rafting Alaskan rivers with my father. They're called standing waves because they stay in one place, where the collision of forces causes them. In rivers, they're behind underwater boulders. In the ocean, they're at the meeting point of opposing currents, usually over shallower water. They're extremely dangerous not just from overall height but from how steep they are and how close together, and I could not avoid them. Even in a ninety-foot sailing yacht, the force of the waves was frightening.

Luckily we had strong engines and were through quickly. By late afternoon, we cleared the lighthouse on the final point. The hills were lush and green, not quite how I had imagined

Morocco. But the water was bright turquoise, the air warm. The African coast would fall steadily away to port, and we'd be in the Canary Islands in three or four days. We couldn't raise our sails yet, since the wind was straight on our nose, but after the Canaries we could run downwind all the way to Mexico. And we'd be arcing south, to catch the trade winds, so we'd soon be able to trade our foul-weather gear for shorts and T-shirts.

That evening the seas increased a bit and the ride was bouncy, but at the time I went below to sleep we were still making eleven knots, very fast time, plowing into each wave with a concussion that sent spray over the pilothouse. All systems were checking out perfectly and the crew were in high spirits.

I fell asleep with Nancy in one of the aft staterooms but was awakened suddenly by a loud metallic popping sound right underneath us. I checked my watch to see it was 1:33 A.M. When things go seriously wrong, you have to keep track of the time.

In the ten seconds it took me to run up on deck, the boat had gone into a spin, the engines still on full, the boat lurching wildly.

"Put the engines in neutral," I yelled, but Emi was panicked and Nick looked stunned. So I pushed them aside and cut the engines myself. The seas were thrown up in jagged shapes by our spin, their edges caught in moonlight. The wooden helm turned idly in my hands, offering no resistance.

Matt came on deck, then Nancy.

"It's the steering or the rudder," I said. "I need to check the hydraulic ram under the bed. Matt, get the emergency tiller."

I went below and took the mattress off, but I couldn't raise the plywood piece under our bed; it was cut too tight. This was why I hadn't checked on the ram before we left. I could hear the rudder banging against the hull and hear wood being ripped apart. I asked Nancy to get Matt and a flathead screwdriver.

When she returned, Matt and I pried the board with two screwdrivers, then Nancy turned on the flashlight and we saw the hydraulic ram disconnected from the fitting on the rudder post. Every time the rudder swung underneath and banged the hull, the fitting on the post tore into the wooden wall separating this stateroom from the next.

"We have to stop the rudder from swinging," I said. "It could open up our hull."

So we went back up on deck. The emergency tiller was heavy iron about eight feet long, with a fitting to attach to the rudder post. Once attached, it swung back and forth with the full force of the huge rudder beneath in large seas. We were not strong enough to stop it. Emi came very close to having her legs crushed between the tiller and the poop deck.

"Tie it off on the winches," I yelled. The wind was over thirty knots and howling.

The others weren't sure what to do, but Matt grabbed a spare halyard and I grabbed a dock line. We caught the end of the tiller, then wrapped the lines around the winches. The big primary winches were strong enough to pull the tiller to the center and hold it there.

"Okay," I yelled over the wind. "We need to go below now and reattach it. Matt, we'll need the big adjustable wrench and some of the larger C-wrenches, twenty-four and above. Emi and Nick, stay up here and make sure those lines stay on the tiller. Nancy, check on Barbara to make sure she's all right."

I was not happy to have one of my lenders onboard. The boat was new, and this kind of thing should not have been happening.

When we went below, we could see the rudder post still moving a bit. So we tried tightening the lines with the winches, but there was no way to get it absolutely still in those seas. This was a problem, because the stainless steel shaft from the hydraulic ram had a threaded end that had to be screwed into the fitting on the rudder post. You can't screw something in unless it's lined up perfectly. I felt the despair I had felt on many occasions that summer and fall since the final stages of building and launch, when the sheer size and weight of the boat presented something too industrial to manage.

But for Matt, who had done hundreds of impossible, shitty tasks in worse weather on purse seiners in southeastern Alaska, this was just another day at the office. He crawled down in with the rudder post and ram, at home with the rumble of the engines and the lurching back and forth in seas, and told me to line up the ram while he held the post in place. So I tried to line up the ram with one hand, ready with a wrench in the other.

We tried a lot of times, timing it with the waves. Matt was grunting and then yelling in frustration, grease on his hands, the fitting slipping and pulling away from him. We came close enough to turn the wrench several times, but the threads wouldn't hold. It had to be lined up perfectly.

Matt's hands and arms were in close to where the fitting kept jerking past the ram; he could have gotten caught between the two pieces of steel. And I didn't know what we would do if we couldn't get the ram reattached. Then Matt yelled "Now!" and I turned the wrench as fast as I could and we had done it. The rudder post was reattached. I tightened the safety, the piece that had somehow failed, and hurried back on deck.

The crew untied the lines on the tiller while I put the engines in gear. I did several tests at slow speed, and everything felt fine. We topped off the steering fluid to be safe, but the steering wasn't slipping. It felt firm. So I bumped the engines back up, though not quite as fast as before, and changed our course for Casablanca. We needed to check the rudder and hull for damage before continuing on to the Canaries. It would be a delay of a day or two but hopefully not more.

Emi and Nick took their watch again, and the rest of us returned to bed, exhausted. I lay awake for a while wondering why I had chosen this kind of life, feeling afraid of the boat, afraid of the wind and sea, afraid of the licenses and permits I would have to apply for again in Mexico, afraid most of all of my bills and debts, especially after the damage Amber had done. If John's loan didn't come through immediately, I wouldn't have enough money even for diesel, or to pay the crew when we arrived. This life I was leading now was in many ways completely irrational, which made it seem plausible that I was doing all of this for unconscious reasons, trying to relive my father's life, for instance, or testing whether I'd kill myself as he had if things got bad enough. There had to be something going on that I wasn't fully aware of, because this was crazy.

I fell asleep finally, and when I awoke, it was only a few hours later to a hideously loud bang beneath me and the same full-speed spin.

On deck, the crew had already cut the engines and Matt was getting the emergency tiller. The wind and seas had come up even more, which was not good.

I went below and looked under the bed, surprised to find the ram still connected. Everything looked fine with the post and its fitting and the ram. "Tell them to turn the wheel all the way to port, then all the way to starboard," I told Nancy, and when they did, I could see the rudder post turn just as it was supposed to, but we were still lurching in circles.

I went back on deck and tried the wheel myself. "We've lost our rudder," I said. I couldn't believe it had happened, but it had. If the steering gear works, but there's no response, and there's no sound of a loose rudder banging the underside of the hull, then there's no rudder down there. Shaped like the tail of an airplane, with the one severed stainless steel post sticking out, it was flying down to the bottom of the ocean.

There was one ship near us on the radar. We could see its lights far off to port. I hailed on the VHF and said we were disabled and needing assistance.

"This is the *Birgit Sabban*. I am not able to give you a tow," the very German voice of the captain came back. "I have limited maneuverability in these seas."

"Please stand by on 16," I told him, and I tried hailing the Moroccan Coast Guard and any other vessels in the area but received no response.

I put the engines in gear and tried steering with them on our previous heading, giving the starboard engine more thrust when I wanted to turn to port, and vice versa. It worked a bit.

The crew were watching me. "That's crazy," Matt finally said. "You can't keep going without a rudder."

"We can steer with the engines," I said.

"Maybe you can," Nick said. "But not us."

They were right, of course. It was crazy. I couldn't steer all the way to Casablanca myself, without help. At slow speed, it would take more than a day to get there, maybe longer. And then, as I was thinking these things, distracted, the boat went into a spin.

"Okay," I said. "You're right. It doesn't make sense to try to steer without a rudder in seas."

"Right-o, then," Nick said in his fake British accent. "At least we've established that."

Everyone grinned. I put the engines back in neutral, then left the helm for the Inmarsat-C station in the main salon. I sent a distress message saying we were disabled, without a rudder, and in need of assistance. Then I returned to the radio.

The German captain was planning to go into the port of Kinitra at daylight, in just an hour or so, to pick up cargo.

"I need you to stay here," I said. "We need assistance. We can't make way consistently in the same direction without our rudder."

"I'll be in radio contact," he said. "I am proceeding now to Kinitra. I will continue to try to reach the Moroccan Coast Guard for you on short-, medium-, and high-frequency radio."

He was leaving us. "You're required by international law to stay and provide assistance," I said. "I have reported the name of your vessel, the *Birgit Sabban,* by Inmarsat-C, and I expect you to remain here."

There was some delay after this. "Okay," he finally said. "We will remain here with you until daylight and then attempt a tow." I thanked him and we waited for daylight.

As we waited, however, the wind and seas kept increasing. The wind was over forty knots and the seas fifteen to eighteen feet. I was using the engines to try to keep our bow into the waves, but I also couldn't stray too far from the German ship and I couldn't keep us straight anyway. Every time we went broadside to the waves we rolled hideously. The waves were a bit too small to be able to capsize us by rolling us over, but it felt close.

The German captain raised the Moroccan Coast Guard on medium-wave radio, but the Moroccans couldn't send out any boats because of the rough weather. All they could offer was a helicopter with a diver, if we wanted to abandon ship. This option would only be possible during daylight.

"We need a tow," I told the German captain. "We need a very long bridle with a shackle, and we need a towline long enough that it will be submerged to absorb shock. We're over one hundred tons."

"Do you have this towline?" he asked.

"No," I said. "Nothing long enough or heavy enough."

"Well, I don't have this equipment either."

"You have long dock lines that are thick enough," I said. "Give us one of those for a bridle, and a shackle if you have it, and then make several lines into a long towline to tie onto it."

"We will see what we have," he said.

Daylight was a dull metallic color in this weather. The German ship was green and three hundred feet long. It made a slow circle and passed in front of us, into the wind and waves.

"I am limited in maneuverability," the captain said. "I can only make a track into the wind and you will have to bring your bow up to my stern."

"I have no rudder," I said.

"This is all I can do, or I will not have control in these seas."

So I used the engines to steer the boat. The wind and seas continued to build, the waves very sharp, becoming twenty-footers packed close together, driven by wind over fifty knots. I could get the boat moving several knots forward, catching up to the freighter, but then my bow would take three feet of solid water over the top and the boat would slough to the side from the impact. The wind would catch us as we came up high over the next twenty-foot wave and blow us into a spin. In the spin, another twenty-footer would catch us broadside and roll us more than fifty degrees, which meant looking down across twenty-one and a half feet of deck more or less straight into the water. Fifty knots of wind has tremendous force. The engines were strong, and I was using all the power they had, but if the wind caught the boat right, there was no stopping the spin without a rudder.

An hour later, when I was finally in position behind the stern of the freighter, I tried to hide in its wind shadow, but it was weaving a bit. The German ship's crew was on the stern, ready to throw small lines with monkey's fists, a knot shaped like a ball. To get close enough for my crew to catch one of these, I would need to place our bowsprit within about twenty feet of the German ship, which was a fearsome sight. The stern of the freighter was fifty feet high and flared on the sides, so that when the stern came down after each wave, it flattened the seas with a loud crash and then a sucking sound as it rose up again. I had to use the engines to keep my bow straight behind the freighter's stern, but I couldn't drift forward any faster than the freighter was going.

I hated to take my hands off the throttles, but I had to radio the other captain. "This is just to verify that you'll be sending a long line to us first, which we will use as a bridle, tying it to both sides of our bow."

"I don't have that line for you. I have only one towline. This is the towline they are throwing to you now."

"But that won't work," I said. "We can't be towed from just one side of the bow. We have to have a bridle."

"You will have to put it in the center."

I couldn't respond because I had to throw the starboard engine hard forward, the port engine hard reverse. The bow straightened but also jumped forward, very close to the freighter's stern, which came down with a huge crash just as two men threw their lines, both of which fell short.

"Put it in the center?" I yelled over the radio. "We have a bowsprit. And we have anchors that will sever the line."

I had to let go of the radio again.

"We are doing our best," the captain said. "We do not have what you are requesting."

"Nancy, go tell the crew this line is it. They have to get it attached through the hole in the bow for the anchors and then to a cleat or the windlass, preferably a cleat." We had enormous steel cleats that were welded to the steel deck underneath the teak.

Nancy worked her way forward along the rail, struggling to hold on amid the spray and storm-force wind.

Our bow went up over a wave just as the freighter's stern drifted to the side, so the wind caught us full blast and spun us, dipping our rail almost to the water. I held on to the throttles and saw the crew holding on to lifelines and keeping so low for balance they were lying on the deck. As we came back around, the boat stalled broadside and I gunned the engines at full power to bring the bow up. I tried not to appear panicked, since Barbara was on deck now. She didn't know how to swim. She was wearing a life jacket, sitting braced against a table, and not saying anything. I didn't like it at all that she or anyone else was experiencing this.

The bow came around under force of the engines, but the trick, with no rudder, was to avoid coming around so fast as to then spin the other way. I had to ease off at the right moment. I succeeded this time, and was able to go straight for a minute and catch up to the freighter, but I was blown in a circle once more before getting the bow up to their stern for another attempt. This time our bowsprit must have come within ten feet of their stern. Completely terrifying. My crew up there and the boat only minimally under my control. Nancy was back beside me, drenched even in her foul-weather gear. She gave me a kiss on the cheek and then watched the crew.

The freighter crew threw lines again, three of them at the same time, which didn't make any sense, but Matt, in a leap on that rolling, pitching deck, right at the lifelines, caught one. He and Nick and Emi hauled the line in and I tried to keep us in position. Tiny, fast adjustments.

They led the line through the gap for the starboard anchor and threw the loop around the cleat just as I was losing the boat to starboard. We were blown sideways away from the freighter as the line played out from their end, and then I saw the freighter crew cleating it off.

"No!" I yelled into the radio. "They can't cleat it off now. They have to let out a long line. It has to be long enough to be submerged. Tell them to take it off! Now!"

Then I yelled to Nancy, "Tell the crew to get away from the bow!"

She ran forward, looking scared, and the captain came back over the radio. "We do not have a longer line," he said.

"You have a longer line!" I yelled. "Give us the goddamn longer line!"

The short line caught tight then and yanked us horrendously to the side, our boat at such a steep angle I thought we might go over. If we hadn't been a sailboat, with heavy keels and built to heel over and recover, we would have been lost. Any motoryacht would have capsized instantly. The crew and Nancy had made it back to midships just in time and were clinging to the lifelines and the seating area. Barbara was under the table, holding one of its legs to keep from flying.

The bowsprit was holding only because it was a monstrously heavy piece of steel. We took several feet of green water, pounding back against the crew, then wallowed for a moment before being yanked through another wave, taking green water again. This severed the line against the flukes of our starboard anchor and we were spinning free of the tow.

"Goddamnit," I said into the radio. "You put my crew and my vessel at risk. Give us a bridle, a long bridle, and then give us a proper towline."

"We will make a turn, go behind you, turn again, and then you may try the tow again. We will search again for a longer line, but I can tell you we do not have what you are requesting."

"With a ship that size, I know you have enough docklines to give us one for a bridle and three more tied together for a long towline."

"We cannot give up all of our dock lines for you. If we lose the lines, or use them to tow you, what do we use when we arrive in port?"

"We'll give them back to you in the harbor as we're taken on by a tug, or a pilotboat can bring you new ones. We have to have a safe towline."

"I cannot risk the security of my vessel. I will give you what I can."

A large wave caught us then from the stern, as the boat was spinning, and I heard a crashing sound. Thousands of gallons dumped onto our aft deck, and our Mediterranean boarding ladder, which was fifteen feet of solid teak and weighed more than five hundred pounds, came loose from its steel mount and began swinging at the stern, ripping off the wooden taffrail and bouncing on its lines.

There was no good way to deal with this. The ladder was heavy enough to crush and kill anyone caught between it and the deck. We had to bring it in before it took out our backstays and our mizzenmast, but it was held high on a halyard and was out of control, too dangerous to approach. I took the halyard and waited for the right timing, for the ladder to swing in over the poop deck. My three crew were ready but kept jumping back out of the way. The deck rolling in the big waves, the wind screaming at over fifty knots, the ladder just one more uncontrollable force until finally it swung in over the poop deck long enough for me to let the halyard go and my crew to pull it forward, where we lashed it down.

I returned to the throttles to face us again into the waves. The boarding ladder was my fault. I should have stowed it on deck before we left Gibraltar. It was necessary for the Mediterranean but only a hazard for an Atlantic crossing. I had been thinking we might need it in the Canary Islands. The hydraulic ram popping loose was my fault, too. I should have checked it. There had been so many things to do before we left Turkey, and I'd been exhausted. I had checked hundreds of other things, but I'd been in a rush and the board beneath the bed wasn't easy enough to remove, because of the bad carpentry. It was also possible that the ram had been sabotaged by a disgruntled crew member or worker during our final days in Turkey, because the safety on the ram should not have failed, and it was hard to imagine how it could have come fully unscrewed across more than six inches of tight threads.

The freighter passed again and I tried to maneuver us closer. The waves remained sharp, their tops blown off in spray, the spray everywhere, filling the air, and the Moroccan Coast Guard still wouldn't send a boat and there were no private boats willing to offer a tow. The freighter was our only option. The Inmarsat-C was supposed to relay distress messages by satellite to ships in our area, but the German ship reported they hadn't seen any notifications.

This second towing attempt was going to be the same horror as the last, I knew. Without a bridle, we couldn't keep the line away from the bowsprit and anchors. The line was heavy dock line for a ship, five-inch-thick nylon, but the force of one hundred tons being yanked through a twenty-foot wave was more than enough to sever it against any kind of edge.

When I finally got our bow up to their stern, the freighter crew threw their lines and one of them wrapped high around our headstay. I watched it wrap around and then the monkey fist dangling there, about ten feet off the deck, just out of reach. And my crew hadn't noticed. They were trying to catch another line. The headstay is the heavy stainless steel wire leading from the end of the bowsprit to the top of the main-mast. It's the main wire holding the mast up. If we fell away from the freighter at this moment, which could very easily happen as our bow came up over a wave and caught the wind, and if the hard yank of the rope on the headstay was enough to make the stay or one of its fittings fail, which was also likely, since the rope was probably rated at about fifteen thou-sand pounds breaking strength, then the mainmast would be pulled down backward onto the deck by its backstays. The mizzen would come down, too, right on top of us.

"Tell them to get that line off my headstay," I told Nancy. "If that line doesn't come off right now, it could pull down our masts. Understand?"

"Oh God," Nancy said, and she ran forward.

It was my most concentrated time on the throttles. I had to keep us close behind their stern. I was surprised to find that I felt not frightened but deeply sad. If I failed, one of my crew or Nancy might be killed as the rigging came down, and it was in fact most likely that I would fail. I couldn't control the wind or waves or the freighter or even my own boat. I stared at that stern and the waves and worked the throttles at revs the engines should never have been subjected to. I could smell the smoke in the exhaust, even in fifty knots of wind. I was willing to destroy my engines. And it took an impossibly long time. The crew didn't understand immediately, and then they saw it and tried to reach it and couldn't, then Matt finally got the boat hook and tried to undo it with that, and the crew on the freighter were not bright enough to give them any slack, but I couldn't leave the throttles to use the radio. Barbara and I were silent. She was staring at the crew, too, and probably thinking similar thoughts. Loss of life and limb, real disaster, was only moments away, and there was nothing more we could do.

Matt caught the line with the boat hook and freed it from the headstay. Seconds later, though I still tried to keep us close to the stern for the towing attempt, our bow was blown hard and fast to starboard and we spun away from the freighter.

I tried to stay calm on the radio as I brought our boat back around for another attempt. "That heaving line was wrapped around my headstay, and none of your crew noticed. They should have cut that line as soon as they saw it wrapped."

"I am up here in the bridge. You will have to notify me of such things."

"I'm trying to steer the boat with only the throttles. My hands aren't free. You tell your first mate to pay some attention and try to avoid getting us killed."

"I have been in contact with the owners, and they have suggested that we tow you from your mainmast. If you have a line you could put around your mainmast, and if we then towed you back the other way to Gibraltar, downwind, it might go easier."

"I can't do that," I said. "My masts are wood, and they're only deck-stepped, so that's not a possible tow point. And I can't have you tow me downwind without a rudder. I'll be powerless to keep from going sideways down a wave, and then I'll get yanked by your short tow rope and the boat will broach. Why don't you just give us the bridle and long towline, which I know you have?"

He didn't answer, and it was time to try moving up to the stern.

My crew caught a line and hauled it in, again with time only to throw it over a cleat and then retreat to midships. Again the terrible yank, the line too short, and the towline severed. It was so stupid.

"Surprise, surprise," I said over the radio. "The short tow-line without a bridle was severed again."

"I am not required to tow you, and we are trying our best."

"You are in fact required to help me, and if you endanger my vessel or crew unnecessarily through not providing the kind of assistance that you could have provided, you are responsible for that also."

"We will try one more time, and then I suggest you take the offer of the helicopter from the Moroccans."

Matt was back in the pilothouse, along with the other crew, and he wanted to talk with me, so I signed off the radio. He looked angry and frustrated, which was a bit frightening with his height and his military haircut, but with him the anger was just a way of getting through the work, nothing personal.

Nick and Emi just looked exhausted and scared. Everyone was soaked.

"What about using chain?" Matt asked. "We could wrap chain around the cleat and put it out past the bowsprit and tie the towline to that. That would keep the line from chafing on the anchors or bowsprit."

It was a good idea. "Will you be able to get the line attached?"

"I think so."

"Okay, let's do it," I said. "But be careful out there. Don't get in the way of anything. Let the boat get hurt, not you."

I radioed the German captain and again asked for the proper equipment, which he again refused. So I told him we were going to try using chain.

As I brought the boat around and worked my way up toward the freighter, Matt wrapped the chain from the starboard anchor around a deck cleat and had a length of about twenty feet going forward through the gap for the anchors.

I was spun several times by the wind, and the freighter crew was not good at throwing lines, but my crew did catch one finally, and Matt somehow attached it to the end of the chain. To this day, I have no idea how he did it, and he did it quickly, while the bow pitched and buried itself in those waves.

My crew retreated to midships, and when the towline came tight with a hard yank that pulled us through a wave, it held. Still a terrible way to be towed, but I hoped it might work. Maybe we'd make it to Casablanca and have a new rudder made, and maybe the delay wouldn't be more than a week. Seemed optimistic, but you never know. Steel is easy and fast to work with, unlike fiberglass or wood.

We were yanked through another wave, several feet of solid water coming over the bow, and in that instant as the water stood above the bow, I was staring at the chain wrapped on the large steel cleat. I was staring at it, and I didn't blink, and the window was clear from just having been drenched, and yet all I saw was that it had vanished. Too quickly for me even to see it go. The steel deck cleat was torn off at its base, the heavy chain was gone, the huge 300-pound anchor was gone, and all that was left was 450 feet of additional chain from the locker flying away at a terrific pace. It caught and severed and we were spinning free, no longer attached. Some of the steel of the bulwarks at the opening for the starboard anchor had been bent outward. Gouges in the teak deck, also, where the deck cleat must have skipped twice. All that damage, all that force. It was too much.

"We're not going to try that again," I said to Nancy and Barbara.

"Wow," Barbara said.

The crew was back in the pilothouse as I called the captain over the radio.

"That took off my deck cleat, anchor, and anchor chain," I told him. "But you couldn't give me any of the equipment I needed when I needed it."

"I recommend accepting the helicopter," he said. "Unless you can continue on your own."

"Stand by, please," I said.

I was still using the throttles, trying to keep our nose into the seas, but my focus now was on the crew and Barbara and Nancy, who were waiting for something from me. Then I decided to just try it again, what the hell. I steered the course for Casablanca with the engines, working hard on the throttles. I went straight for a minute or two, then spun again.

"Okay, never mind," I said. "We've been trying this for ten hours. I haven't left the throttles for ten hours." It was amazing. Each hour I had thought it couldn't get worse, and each hour it had. "We can only get the helicopter during daylight, which is only about two more hours, but really a bit less in this weather. Let me check our position again for a second."

I went to the chart and plotted our position while Matt used the engines to try to keep us into the waves. The waves were just big enough and steep enough to roll and capsize us if one hit exactly right while we were sideways in the trough.

"We're only about fifteen miles from land," I said. "Sixty miles from Casablanca, but only fifteen from land, which means we could drift enough during the night to go aground in high surf. I can't keep the boat going straight under power, which means I can't control the boat or guarantee we won't drift into land. We're not on fire, and we're not sinking. The boat is still seaworthy."

"Ha," Barbara said.

"We are still seaworthy," I said. "Because we're not on fire or taking on water. But I can't think of any other options right now. I can't figure out how to make this work. We can't get a tow, we can't make our own way, and it's not safe to just wait for better weather or a better chance at a tow, because night is coming and we're too close to land and these seas are big enough to capsize us and may get bigger."

I was starting to repeat myself, I knew. It was because I was getting choked up. The feeling came out of nowhere. It was the thought of having to tell my crew that we would be abandoning ship, something I had never imagined I would say. I wonder if any captain really believes he or she will ever have to give that order. It was almost impossible to speak. "I think we have to abandon ship," I said. "I don't think the helicopter is that great an idea, either, and I always thought it would be safest to stay with the boat, even if it was swamped, but I can't guarantee your safety onboard anymore, so it's time to get off."

No one looked happy, but no one disagreed, either.

I called the German captain. "Please call the Moroccan Coast Guard and ask them for the helicopter as soon as possible."

He asked for confirmation and I gave it.

"David?" Barbara asked. "How do we get onto the helicopter?"

"They drop a diver into the water and then we get into the water one at a time and they lift us up on a harness or in a basket, with the diver helping us while we're in the water."

"I don't swim."

"I know. You'll be wearing a life jacket, and the diver will help you."

"I won't be able to see, either, without my glasses."

I didn't know what to say to her. It was terrible.

"You have to promise me you'll go with me, David. If you'll go into the water with me, I'll do it."

I thought about that. It meant I'd be in the water the whole time she was being lifted up. I couldn't help but think of sharks. I've always been unreasonably afraid of them. "Okay," I said. "I can't think of why not. We'll have to be the last two, and I'll help you swim to the diver."

"You promise?"

"I promise."

We had to wait about twenty minutes for the helicopter. Everyone trying to think of what he or she needed to take, heading below to collect things.

"You can't take your stuff," I said. "It will weigh you down in the water. So no one takes anything except maybe a wallet."

Matt relieved me at the throttles while I sent another distress message on the Inmarsat saying we were abandoning ship. Then I set off the Inmarsat's alarm and the Emergency Position Indicating Radio Beacon (EPIRB) so we could track the boat. And I called the German captain, who verified the helicopter was on its way. I was worried about the helicopter. So many helicopters went down in storms, and our boat was still seaworthy. We were still safely aboard it. The weather was even starting to die down, the wind just over forty knots, but that didn't mean it wouldn't come right back up. The weather reports weren't telling us much. I was also worried about salvage rights. If I stayed on board, no one could claim salvage rights, but if I left, anyone could claim the boat, I believed. I wasn't completely sure.

"I keep thinking I should stay with the boat," I told everyone in the pilothouse. "So no one can claim salvage rights."

"David," Barbara said. "You promised. You're coming with me."

"Sorry," I said. "I'm not thinking straight. It's just that if I lose this boat, I've lost everything. Even if I get a full payout on the insurance, I owe more than that in the business and I have no way back." It was stupid to be talking aloud about all of this, I knew, but I couldn't help it. I've never been great at keeping my own counsel.

"The boat's not worth it," Barbara said. "You're making the right decision. And you'll find a way back. I know you will."

I didn't believe her, of course. I felt beat.

I got on the radio with the German captain. "Do you know how salvage rights work?" I asked him. "If I get off the boat, can the next person who climbs on board claim the boat?"

"I'm not sure," he said. "I'm not sure what all of the laws say."

"Okay," I said. "Then I'd like to notify you and anyone else hearing this, notifying all stations that I am not giving up any rights to this vessel. I intend to come back in another boat tomorrow and get back on board. I am getting off the boat now only to assist with the safety of my crew and passengers, but I am not abandoning the vessel."

There was no response from the German captain or from any other station. I hailed the German captain again and made arrangements to use his life raft, in case the helicopter plan didn't work. Then I was talking to the crew about the helicopter versus the life raft. I don't think anyone wanted to hear, but I felt I needed to warn them. "The sides of the ship are pretty high, so there's some risk there on the rope ladder, but otherwise the life raft is safer. The helicopter is definitely riskier. Sometimes they go down in storms."

Nancy looked at me and I could tell I should shut up. I was not exactly reassuring Barbara or the crew. So I shut up.

The German captain came on over the radio and said we should see the helicopter any minute, and then we heard it and saw it coming in low. I took my handheld VHF onto the aft deck to talk with the pilot.

I called the helicopter on the VHF but didn't get a response. They were hovering close enough that I could see the pilot and copilot, so I held my VHF in the air and pointed at it and tried hailing them again, but nothing happened, so I went back to the helm and tried on the mounted VHF. The German captain came back instead.

"They do not have a radio onboard," he said.

"The rescue helicopter doesn't have a VHF?"

"No," he said. "They do not have a VHF or any other kind of radio."

I looked around at my crew. "A Coast Guard rescue helicopter out in a storm for an abandon ship and they don't bring a radio."

"So much for the Moroccans," Nick said.

"Well shit-o," Matt said, trying to do Nick's Brit voice.

So we waited and watched as they lowered their diver down on a cable. The cable had a small step, too small to see.

"No basket," I said. "It looks like we have to stand on that cable. We'll be clipped in, too, I'm sure. Make sure you're clipped in and that the diver checks everything."

The diver had to swim a hundred feet upwind toward us, into the waves. He had fins, a mask, and a snorkel, but he was struggling. You could see quite a belly underneath his wet suit, and his arms were thin. We had an out-of-shape diver rescuing us, without a radio.

When he was within about thirty feet, he motioned for us to come, so Matt gave Emi a last hug, said "Here goes," and jumped in. He swam out quickly to the diver and then they both swam a bit farther away from the boat, the diver holding on to Matt to help him. The ocean was dark green and gray in the overcast light, streaky with spray. The wind and seas had died down but were still high.

The helicopter came closer, but not close enough, and I was confused about what the diver was doing. He and Matt were just floating there. This went on for some time. Meanwhile, we were drifting toward them. We were rolling enough in the seas that our large steel hull presented a danger to them if we came too close. And our ninety-foot mainmast, swinging in long arcs, was a hazard for the helicopter.

The diver was having trouble. He seemed tired. Matt was supporting him in the waves, helping him. And then the diver pointed at our boat, gave Matt a weak push toward us, and swam the other way toward the helicopter.

We couldn't believe it. The diver was saving himself, leaving Matt in the water. Emi was the first to yell and start looking for a line. We all scrambled for lines to toss overboard for Matt.

"Swim toward the bow!" I yelled to Matt. "Around the bow to the boarding ladder!" I didn't know whether he could even hear us in forty knots of wind. We couldn't bring him up on the port side. There was no ladder, and he could be pushed under by the rolling of the hull.

Emi was frantic. Nick and Nancy and Barbara were all

grabbing lines, too. We had several docklines and several halyards overboard for Matt. I was afraid to use the engines because I might just make things worse. I could run him over or send us too far away, or wrap a line on a prop.

Matt was swimming hard for the bow as we drifted down onto him. He caught a line that Emi and Nick led under the bowsprit from the starboard side, so he was able to hold on to this as he swam, and he cleared the bow. He kept holding on, and stayed close to the boat, Emi and Nick pulling him aft toward the boarding ladder. Then I threw him a life ring attached to a line, and he grabbed on to that. Someone lowered the boarding ladder, I'm not sure who. Emi went down the ladder as Matt came close, and she grabbed him by the collar of his life jacket to help him onto the lower step, which was plunging into the seas, and then up the other steps onto the deck.

Matt was exhausted. We all went back inside the pilot-house. The helicopter had vanished.

"We're going to need that life raft," I told the German captain.

"It is already inflated and towed behind us. Can you see it?"

It was raining hard and the visibility was bad, but the ship was not far away, and I could just make out the orange raft.

"Thank you," I said. "Are you going to come around with it?"

"I am turning into the wind now. You will need to come to it."

"Make sure all the lines are up," I told my crew. "I don't want a line around a prop."

In a few minutes, they reported the lines were up, and I engaged the engines, trying to go straight. The life raft was about five hundred yards away and moving at several knots.

As I closed the gap, I told the crew what the procedure would be. "I'll try to put the raft beside our stern on the starboard side. I'll come in close and hit reverse and that should pull our stern close. Matt will be the first one in, if you're feeling up for it. Can you jump holding a line and then tie it off?"

Matt nodded.

"Okay, Matt jumps in first with the line, and Nick holds on

to the line from our deck. Wrap it around a shroud so you're not holding all of the weight. Then it will be Emi, then Nancy. Then it will be Barbara. I'm sorry I won't be jumping with you, but you'll have lots of area to jump into, and Matt and Emi and Nancy will be there to help."

"Okay," Barbara said.

"Then I'll take the line from Nick and Nick will jump in. Then I'll jump in, bringing the line with me. Okay?"

I was having trouble bringing the bow around to get up to the raft. One of the lines had wrapped around my props.

"Fill the ditch bag," I said. "You can bring your most valuable items, just a few things, whatever will fit in the bag along with the emergency stuff that's already in there. We can toss it in after Matt. But you only have the next five minutes or so to do it."

I was having a lot of trouble with the engines, having to punch the throttles to get anything out of the props. It was getting dark and this was our last chance before we'd have to get into our own life raft, and I didn't know how the freighter would pick us up in our own raft. In these seas, we could be killed if we floated under their stern.

"Come on," I said. "Come on." I asked the captain if he could let out the line a bit more, but he said that was all there was. I asked Nancy to put the portable VHF in a baggie and then in my foul-weather gear pocket, and I had my knife. The others were done gathering their things and were waiting on deck. The EPIRB and Inmarsat were flashing red and beeping. It was a scene I hadn't imagined I would ever see.

"Let's rehearse the order," I said, and everyone called out what they would do and when. "Make sure your lights are turned on and working, make sure you have a whistle."

It took much too long to get up to the raft. The props were badly fouled. But the life raft did get closer, and closer, and finally I was within a hundred feet of it. I brought the bow in, almost ran it over, and hit reverse.

"Go now!" I yelled. I ran from the helm to the rail and saw

that the raft was touching us. Matt was already in, tying off the line.

"It's on!" he yelled, and Emi threw the ditch bag. Then she jumped. It was about ten feet down to the raft. She hit right in the center. The raft had a partial enclosure on the top, and Matt and Emi were trying to untangle themselves from it to leave room for the next.

"Now Nancy." And Nancy was in, then scrambling to get out of the way, then Barbara jumped with a yell and was fine, then I grabbed the line from Nick. His foot caught on the wooden rail as he jumped, so that he spun forward in the air and landed on his face at the edge of the raft, his legs in the water. The others pulled him aboard. I unwrapped the line and jumped, trying not to land on anyone.

And that was it. We had abandoned ship. I sat there in the raft, in the storm, and watched my boat float away. It was rocking wildly from side to side, the dark wooden masts arcing low to one side then the other, but it was not taking on any water. It could rock in those seas forever, it seemed, and yet I had abandoned it.

We were being pulled in by the freighter's crew. I took the VHF out of my pocket, protected in its baggie, and talked with the captain.

"Please be sure to keep us well away from the stern," I said, and he said he would. I could see his crew with the line going forward over the deck to pull us from midships and keep us clear. They had a rope ladder over the side with wide wooden rungs. I felt only sad, and tired, not excited or scared. But I still had the task of getting the crew safely on board. This was why I couldn't have stayed with my boat. The side of the freighter was lower than the stern but still high, and when it rolled away from us, we'd see thirty or forty feet of steel, and then it would roll back down at us. Barbara was overweight, without a lot of upper-body strength, and she couldn't see without her glasses, and she couldn't swim.

"I'll help you at the ladder," I told Barbara. "I'll climb on behind, but you need to get your feet onto a rung quick and don't let go for anything. We have to time it for when the ship rolls toward us. Grab the ropes then and get your feet on a rung immediately. Then the ship will swing away and you'll be lifted from the water. Once you're on, keep moving up, and their crew will help you. Nick will come after me, but otherwise we'll use the same order for climbing the ladder that we used for jumping into the raft. Matt will be our guinea pig, as always."

"Call me chum," Matt said.

Up close, it was pretty frightening. The ship rolled a hell of a lot, and sucked at the water. "Keep your arms and legs inside the raft!" I yelled. My crew were trying to push off the ship when we were sucked in close. "The raft can take it."

The ladder was made of crappy old rope and chewed-up wooden rungs. And the rolling was so extreme that the ladder would stay close for only a second or two before it was yanked high into the air away from us. I didn't know if Barbara would make it. I wasn't strong enough to hold her on if she wasn't holding on well herself.

Matt went first, catching hold fast and then yanked upward, his feet slipping. He was strong enough to hold on, but I was glad Barbara had her glasses off and couldn't see what it looked like. Emi went next, grabbing the ladder late because we were thrown by a wave, but she caught it and had no problem once she was climbing. The crew pulled her onboard and now she and Matt were looking down at us from the rail, shouting encouragement.

Nancy grabbed the ladder, but we were thrown so hard to the side, swirling past it, that she couldn't hold on and was pulled out of the raft before she let go. This put her in the water between the raft and the steel hull, and I felt the sudden panic of losing her. In an instant, it was clear how much I loved her. Nick and I lunged for her and pulled her back in just before the raft rubbed up against the steel.

"Oh God," Nancy said. "That wasn't good at all."

"I'm sorry," I said.

She was more hesitant the next time, so we waited for several waves, and then she caught one, climbed, and was pulled aboard.

That meant it was Barbara's turn.

Nick and I were talking her through it, one of us on either side, holding the ladder when we could and waiting for a good wave.

"I think it's going to be the next one," I said. "Get ready to grab on quick and get your feet onto a rung."

The wave came, we were lifted high up against the ladder, and she grabbed on, but the wave pushed us to the side and I fell, holding on to the ladder with only one hand. Nick had fallen, too. Barbara stepped onto the rungs just as the ship lurched away from us. I managed to get one hand up to push on her backside, but I wasn't there behind her on the ladder as I had promised. Both of her hands were holding a wooden rung, not nearly as good as holding on to ropes, and her feet were on a rung not far below, so that she wasn't standing up straight but was in a crouch. The boat was heaving very hard, with a lot of force to fling her off. I didn't think she was going to make it, and I was ready to try to catch her, but I was afraid she would slide down the hull and be pushed underwater as it rolled back.

Then I heard Barbara growl. It was a low, guttural growl, a primal refusal to die, and she held on and climbed up to the next rungs, and by the time the ship had rolled back toward us, the freighter crew and my crew were pulling her aboard.

"Oh God," I said. I was so grateful.

Barbara hugged the crew on deck, and we waited a minute or two, collecting ourselves, then the ship rolled close and Nick climbed up the ladder, and when it rolled close again, I went, holding a line to pull up the ditch bag, and we were safe.

THE FREIGHTER CREW, all from Kiribati in the South Pacific, were warm in their welcome, and the two Germans, the captain and first mate, were gracious. We were given their own dry clothing and excellent quarters. I didn't change but went up to the bridge and looked at my boat, half a mile away now, still heaving back and forth. It looked small from here, but riding high off the water. I couldn't grasp that I had lost the boat, that it was no longer mine. I still hoped I would somehow get back on board. But most of all I was grateful that no one had been hurt. We were all safe, and the only issue now was property, which is only money.

I was thinking also, though, of the time when a captain I had hired had abandoned *Grendel* near the Guatemalan border with its engine destroyed. I'd had to replace that engine with no facilities, no marina even, and it had taken almost four months to get the boat out of there.

The captain told me he would circle my boat all night, to keep it safe from pirates. He showed me on the radar. A ring of small vessels about three miles out, waiting. Moroccan fishermen who would come aboard to strip the electronics and anything else they could use. I was surprised at his interest, having assumed he would continue on to Kinitra, his intended port, as soon as we were aboard. But he had given up on Kinitra, and said he would try to tow my boat in the morning if the seas died down. He would tow it ninety miles back to Gibraltar.

I didn't say anything at the time, standing in the bridge with the captain, but I knew what was going on. Now that I had abandoned ship, he was going to claim salvage rights. I wondered if we would suddenly see better towing gear, and I wondered if he had pulled this scam before.

The captain was a deliberate man, in his fifties, sitting at his comfortable helm seat and chain smoking. He was dressed in a white shirt and gray slacks, as if he were at the office. He spoke almost perfect English, as did his first mate. The bridge was quiet and dark, the sound of the strange two-cylinder diesel like a great vacuum pump far below. He steered with a small joystick, just tiny adjustments to circle my boat. His claims about only being able to go upwind in a straight line seemed not quite true.

"*Ich kann ein bischen Deutsch*," I said. I spoke a bit in German about hiking in the mountains of Germany and visits with my German grandfather to the *konditerei* (the bakery) for sweets. The captain indulged me and spoke of boyhood treks and blueberries.

We slipped back into English to discuss the Moroccans and their lack of a VHF. He had never heard back from the Moroccan Coast Guard.

He had also contacted my insurance company, as I had. I assumed the owners of the ship would try to recover towing fees, and I suspected they would ask for some outrageous payment for salvage rights. I wanted to know whether the first mate or captain had ever been involved in this before. "Have you ever rescued any other boats?" I asked.

"Yes," the captain said. "Another sailboat, a similar size as yours."

So this captain had known what he was doing. I felt sure he would produce better towing equipment in the morning.

I said good night and descended to our quarters to change out of my wet clothes and take a hot shower. The freighter crew had invited my crew to watch a video about their home in Kiribati, but everyone had said no because they were tired. They were stretched out in dry clothes in a small sitting area eating lunch meat and crackers.

I woke several times that night. The captain and his first mate were taking turns on the watches. Neither of them seemed inclined to speak. They had more or less the same attitude. Whichever one was awake would sit smoking and making small steering adjustments in a manner that looked contemplative, as if trying the joystick for the first time, over and over. The glances at the large radar screen below, showing my boat and the ring of Moroccan fishermen/pirates, the glances at depth and radios, then more of staring three hundred feet to the bow light and beyond. The slow rolling and the vacuum pump sound of the diesel. I had no idea how they could spend years like this. I suppose it was peaceful and ordered and safe.

We could see the masthead light on my boat, arcing back and forth. I had turned it on at the end to keep the boat visible, and I had left the engines and electrical system running so that all systems would stay up, bilge pumps included. I had no idea what to hope for, whether for complete loss or recovery or something else. I was so tired, and no matter what happened, my original plans were stretched and broken. The idea of getting to Mexico on time to run my winter charters, after first sorting out the salvage mess and then getting a new rudder and probably finding new crew, seemed remote. Finding money to pay the $3,000 deductible and anything not covered by insurance, and finding money to pay the lenders and all the bills, was still the largest worry, worse by far than losing my rudder at sea. If the loan promised by John didn't come in, I was going to go under, despite the recent loan from Rand and Lee. There wasn't enough time to raise $150,000 from other sources. Especially once word got around about the lost rudder and the canceled winter schedule. It seemed like I had already failed, and was just hanging on to make sure it was real.

In the morning, I climbed down into the life raft with the first mate and one of the crew from Kiribati. My own crew had to stay on board. The captain explained to me that his company was now responsible for the boat, liable for it because of their salvage claim, and my crew was not allowed on board. They were letting me on, though, because they had to have someone who knew the boat. Placed into the raft with us was a hundred-foot bridle of very thick dock line, exactly what I had requested the day before.

The freighter circled more deftly than it had before and brought the life raft close. The seas and wind had died down considerably. They had not blown my boat onto land during the night, obviously, which meant that we could have stayed aboard, though in that case the freighter probably would not have stayed with us all night.

When we came close to the stern rail of my boat, I climbed aboard quickly, the first back on deck. I considered telling the other two to stay in the raft, refusing to let them board, but I hesitated and they climbed up after me. I needed help with the towline, and I needed the tow. I was too tired to think clearly. I wonder now what would have happened. Would they have fought me to come aboard? Would the captain have refused to help me afterward and let me drift? Or would I have won the day, handling the towlines myself and avoiding the salvage claim? I have no idea.

What happened was that they came aboard and we tied the bridle to the bows. They even gave me a large shackle so that when the towline was thrown to us we would be able to simply slip the shackle over and screw in the pin.

I couldn't steer up to the freighter's stern reliably with fouled props, and the German captain didn't want that anyway. He was happy to pull his freighter alongside, close enough to throw a line across our deck. It's true the seas were much calmer, the wind much lower, but what the captain was willing to do had also changed considerably.

I called him on the radio. "I see you have all of the equipment you said you didn't have."

"The conditions have changed," he said. "We were unable to provide other assistance in the sea conditions that prevailed yesterday."

"You're a liar," I said. "And a criminal. You put my crew and my boat at risk. You went for the salvage claim. You are not going to get away with this."

There was a pause, then he came back on the radio. "My instructions are to tow you to Gibraltar. Are you willing to help ensure the safety of the vessel during that tow?"

"Yes I am, you sonofabitch."

"Thank you, then. Please stand by on 16."

The towline he used was five times the length he had offered us the day before. It was long enough that the middle section stayed slack in the water the entire time, absorbing shock. It was exactly what we had needed.

To keep the boat from crawfishing side to side, we dragged dock lines, a sea anchor (a kind of underwater parachute) with a big hole cut in it, and two plastic kayaks, which swamped and darted back and forth under the surface like green lures. With all of this trailing from the stern, the boat sawed back and forth very little, and we were able to reduce the chafing of the towlines at the bows.

The tow went smoothly for the day and a half back to Gibraltar. The first mate puked a few times, seasick, then sat on the poop deck and smoked. The man from Kiribati puked a few times then slept in the pilothouse. I fixed canned meals and amused myself with the Inmarsat. To get it to stop beeping, I had to cut its power. When I brought it back up, there were finally some response messages, asking me to verify that I had set off the Inmarsat distress alarm and my EPIRB. "Just a bit late," I typed. "I'm being towed to Gibraltar now."

Then I sent an e-mail to Seref. "We've lost our rudder near Casablanca. It fell off. I can't possibly express to you how disappointed I am in this boat. I'm not paying another dime. No commission or tip. But you've already collected your commissions, haven't you?"

I checked the engine room, then turned off the engines. Everything seemed fine down there. The main salon and galley, however, were a wreck after the night of rolling. The contents of the refrigerator had spilled across the salon floor, which luckily was teak, like the deck outside, and could be cleaned. Dishes had flown out of the dishwasher and broken. Everything we had stowed under the salon desk had come loose.

The weather, always ready with a new insult, had become clear and sunny. The seas had steadily dropped, and by the time we made Gibraltar, they were almost flat.

I had banged my knee on something during the previous day's towing attempts, and since then it had stiffened. By the time we began the tow, I was hobbling, and by the time we reached Gibraltar, I basically couldn't walk. I wasn't sure how the whole knee thing had happened.

As we entered the Bay of Gibraltar, the German captain and I were busy on the radio making plans. He would dock first and then a tugboat would moor us alongside. In the meantime, we needed to retrieve the items dragging behind. I hobbled as best as I could to help, but the first mate did most of the cutting, letting the crew member from Kiribati do most of the hauling, and the cutting was indiscriminate. By the time I yelled out, he had cut one of the kayaks free, which now was drifting out of the Bay of Gibraltar.

"You won't do anything more on this boat without my permission," I told him. "This is still my boat, and I'm still the captain."

"No you're not," he said. "You can fuck off, as you Americans like to say. You're going to bring me a nice income."

"Income?" I asked.

"The first mate receives five percent, and the captain receives ten percent. That's from the salvage claim. We also receive a bonus if the towing charges are more than the cargo from Kinitra."

"You're a criminal," I said.

"The captain and I are smart," he said, "and you are not. Poor little stupid American, out on the high seas. It's a big world, isn't it?"

As it turned out, that was to be one of the more pleasant encounters of the day. There is an outer wall of the Gibraltar harbor called Impound Island, which is where the larger arrested ships are kept. Enormous rusting hulks from third world countries, abandoned. Being towed past them by a freighter was like looking at my own failure, perfectly manifested. A dream and the empty hull left over when it dies.

Once the *Birgit Sabban* had docked, a tug pulled us close. My crew and Nancy and Barbara waved down at me, looking showered and well rested. But before I could tie off, the man from Kiribati climbed onto my lifelines and leapt for the freighter. He caught the edge of the deck and dangled from the freighter's side. I looked down at the thin strip of water sucking between our hulls. If he fell, he was most likely going to die. And I had no control over my boat. The other Kiribati crew and my crew on the deck of the *Birgit Sabban* rushed to help him, grabbing at his blue jumpsuit and the backs of his arms. A confusion of movement and yelling, but they pulled him aboard.

The German first mate standing beside me laughed. "He thinks your boat is cursed. Maybe he is correct."

We tied off to the freighter, exchanged crew, and then the German captain informed me that the admiralty marshal of Gibraltar was coming to arrest the boat. My insurance company and the shipping company had not come to immediate agreement, so my boat would be put under twenty-four-hour guard, and I was responsible for paying for the guard. This was becoming so bad so fast, I decided to contact the law firm in Gibraltar that had set up my company and registered the boat.

We didn't have a phone onboard, so I would have to wait until after I was arrested. While I was waiting, the German captain came by and handed me his cell phone with a call from my insurance company representative. The woman sounded friendly, but I told her I wanted to consult my lawyers.

"Why would you need to do that?" she asked. "Did you do something wrong?"

"No," I said. "But I don't like being arrested. I don't feel well represented."

"We are here to represent you. You must cooperate with us if you want us to consider coverage of your claim. We need a full written account of what happened, and we'll send a surveyor to assess the damage. The boat will need to be hauled out. But first you must tell me what happened."

"I look forward to working with you," I said, "after I talk with my lawyers. In the meantime, if you could keep the boat from getting arrested, that would be a plus."

Barbara was a lawyer, with her own firm in Colorado, and she agreed with this approach. "You have to be careful," she told me. The boat was her asset, too, as one of the lienholders. "We'll get through this, David. It will all work out okay."

My crew were only slightly less anxious than the man from Kiribati to leave the boat, but we had to wait for the admiralty marshal. Nancy was the only one who would stay with me in the end, I knew. There's an enormous comfort in knowing you won't be left completely alone to wade through unfortunate circumstances. When I'd had problems with *Grendel* in Mexico,

I'd been alone, and that had definitely made it worse. I knew that if and when I sailed out of Gibraltar again to cross the Atlantic, Nancy would be with me.

At the moment, Nancy was worried about my knee and made me promise we'd see a doctor as soon as possible.

When the admiralty marshal finally arrived, he was kind and apologetic. I was not personally under arrest, only the vessel. It would be moved to one of the marinas and placed under twenty-four-hour guard, with only the crew allowed to board. The documents I had to sign made it clear the boat was no longer mine, but was in the possession of the admiralty, so I asked about insurance.

"We will take out a temporary insurance policy today," he said.

"And who will pay for that?" I asked.

"I'm afraid those costs will have to be recouped, also, sir."

The admiralty marshal could do nothing but apologize, and I didn't press, since he wasn't a bad guy. He posted a notice on one of our pilothouse windows saying the boat had been arrested, then left.

Only Queensway Quay, the crappiest marina in Gibraltar, could take us, and that was along a seawall, not an actual slip. I didn't have a choice. The boat wasn't mine anymore, and the marshal had required it be moved immediately. Queensway Quay arranged a tow, and I knew this would be part of my bill, too.

This towboat was small, about forty feet, with two crew on board. They came alongside and arranged a bridle at the bow, short trucking straps with a shackle. I wasn't happy about how close the shackle was. It was going to bang against my bow.

"That's all we got, mate," the captain of the tow said.

I limped back to the pilothouse and hoped for the best. My crew cast off our lines and the towboat captain just took off. He hadn't judged the wind or current or done anything to help us spring away from the freighter, so we were pulled along its side with our shrouds scraping, then past the bow at about ten knots, missing the next ship, moored directly ahead, by only a few feet.

"What are you doing?" I asked the captain on the VHF. "I don't need any more damage. Try taking it easy and thinking a little."

"I've driven towboats all my life, mate. I know what I'm doing."

"You scraped us along that freighter and almost slammed us into the next ship at high speed."

"Almost, mate. That's the operative word here. Almost. No harm done."

I was at the helm but I couldn't do anything. I had tried to start my engines to assist with the tow, but they weren't starting for some reason. I suspected the batteries were low, though I wasn't sure how that could have happened. I would have to worry about it later. No one was allowing any time for it now.

The captain towed us at high speed, then abruptly stopped. He had to check something, and he and his mate weren't even looking up as we drifted very quickly.

"Someone get on the bow and yell at him," I said. "We're going to run him over."

I tried hailing on the VHF, but the captain wasn't near his radio, so I followed Matt and the others to the bow. Sinking a towboat would probably look interesting. By the time I had hobbled up there, though, Matt had yelled and the captain ran forward to slam both throttles. He made it out from under my bow just in time.

"Christ," I said to Matt. "When does it end?"

"It never ends, David. It's a boat."

As we entered the tiny marina, we were drifting to the side in current. The captain did a pretty decent job, though, of pulling us in a tight circle to place us against a high stone wall.

I was not happy about this wall. It looked as if it would smash us if there were any surge. I called Queensway Quay again on the VHF and asked if they had anything else, but they didn't. Because of the boat's size, this was the only space available in all of Gibraltar.

A thin guy came down the dock and warned us about surge. He lived on a sixty-foot tug parked inland from us on the same wall. "It comes in hard," he said. "For just a short time, but it'll knock the piss out of you."

We were already using all of our fenders and spring lines, so he came back with some old tires that we roped up and hung over the side, too. A very friendly guy. Matt and Emi headed off with him, I think to share a pint. Nick went looking for a phone, and Nancy and I visited the marina office, asking again to be moved or to borrow some larger fenders, both of which they refused.

When we returned to the boat, Barbara wasn't back, and the admiralty marshal's guard hadn't shown up, and I didn't want to ignore my knee any longer, so we went looking for the hospital.

Gibraltar's a gloomy place, always cloudy because of the Rock. Nancy and I had grown oddly fond of it, mostly because of one restaurant pub called the Clipper, which serves heaping portions of comfort food. Chicken pie with mash and peas, that sort of thing. But I felt like an outcast now, unable to pay my bills, under arrest, invalid, brought back under tow when I should have been in the Caribbean.

We took a taxi up a steep hill and then had several flights of stairs. The hospital was small and grim, as they are everywhere except the United States, where they are large and grim. The doctor was Indian. He prodded and rotated my knee, which made me yelp more than once, sending sharp pains all through my leg and into my stomach, and then told me it was just a nasty infection from the cut I had on my knee. If I had taken the time to apply a bit of Neosporin during the towing incident, I would have been fine. But of course I hadn't even noticed the cut whenever it happened. He gave me a topical and an antibiotic and said I'd be walking normally in twenty-four hours.

We took another taxi back down to the harbor, and as I hobbled out to the dock with Nancy, Barbara rushed up to us. "You're not going to like what you see, David," she said. "I'm so sorry. I told the marina, and they've brought another fender, but the damage is already done."

As we neared the boat, I could see that a twenty-foot section of the port rail had been bashed against the wall so hard the fenders had been ripped off and the steel bulwarks bent in. The teak rail had been smashed to pieces and the stanchions bent at odd angles. Paint had been taken off the hull in some places and bare steel showed through. We had been gone only forty-five minutes, and it was already calm again. It was incredible.

"Fuck," I said. There wasn't much else to say. It was much more damage than we had taken from the towing attempts.

The other crew came back in the next couple of hours, just after dark, and said similar things.

"Well at least it's not my boat right now," I told them. "It belongs to the admiralty, and the damage should be covered by their insurance policy. They'd better cover it. And where is this twenty-four-hour guard?"

Nancy and I sat in the pilothouse, which was a gorgeous place, with large windows, dark mahogany, and plenty of comfortable seating around two tables. I just wanted to sit for a while. The crew were gathering laundry and taking care of their own business. I knew I would lose them. It would probably take a month to work out this mess and get a new rudder, maybe longer.

"There are the engines, too," I told Nancy. "I have to work on that tomorrow, figure out why they're not starting."

"I want to be back home," she said. "I mean I'm not going, I'll stay here with you, but doesn't this suck?"

"It does suck," I said.

We decided to get dinner at one of the restaurants on the dock. It would cost us at least $10 or $15 each, but what the hell. It had been an awful day. We met Barbara walking back from the phones, and she joined us.

"This is good," Barbara said. "We need something normal. Just forget the boat exists. It isn't there."

"What boat?" Nancy asked.

"Okay, okay," I said. We ordered and I drank some water and looked at the clean maroon tablecloth, the candles, the white cloth napkins, my water glass.

Then Nick walked up to us, holding the back of his head with one hand. "David," he said. "I hit my head pretty bad. I didn't know the hatch was open in the galley, and I fell down into the engine room." He removed his hand from the back of his head and showed us the blood.

It was a bit much to believe, but there it was.

The restaurant called us a cab, and Nick and I went outside to wait. I told Barbara and Nancy to stay and have dinner. I made sure I had money, and I knew where the hospital was. While we waited for the cab, I kept him talking, making sure he stayed lucid.

"I'm not dead yet," he said. "Head wounds bleed a lot. They look worse than they are."

"That's true," I said. "But we need to be careful. We'll wake you up every hour or so tonight, or whatever schedule the doctor recommends. And you have to keep talking, so I know you're fine. Let me know if you feel dizzy or faint or anything happens to your vision or you feel like you're going to fall."

"Keep saying stuff like that and I might." But he had his lopsided grin that was part of why we all liked him so much.

"Sorry," I said. "I won't let them take your organs until it looks pretty final."

"Cheers, mate."

I had him sit on the curb, so that if he fell it wouldn't be far, and we waited. The cab was taking forever. Endless headlights and small cars zooming past on the narrow street, but no cab stopping.

"Well shit-o," Nick said.

"Indeed," I said.

I asked if he'd be okay for a minute, and he said he would, so I rushed back the hundred feet or so to the restaurant and asked them to call the cab again. When I returned, Nick was still fine, still sitting there.

"Your dad will never forgive me," I said. First the trip on *Grendel* up the coast from San Francisco, a nightmare of seasickness and mechanical breakdowns, pounding for three days into fifteen-foot seas and thirty-five-knot winds just to get to Eureka, where Charlie and Nick wisely disembarked and took a bus. Then the paint had fallen off the hull this summer during Charlie's *Odyssey* course. Now this. His son had taken a semester off from Oberlin to crew from Turkey to Mexico after I'd filled him full of tropical visions, and here we'd only made it to Morocco before losing our rudder, and then Nick had fallen ten feet onto steel beams just for icing.

"My mom's the one who won't forgive you," he said.

"Oh great."

"Just pulling the old leg, mate. The 'rents will be okay."

The cab finally came and we made it to the hospital, where the doctor, a different one from earlier in the day but also Indian, said it would probably be fine. Some painkillers, an antibiotic, and if we wanted to wake Nick all night on coma alert, we could, but it probably wasn't necessary.

Nick called his parents, I promised we'd wake him every hour, and we were back on the street.

"No more events tonight," I said. "This day has gone on long enough."

I **WOKE NICK** every hour that night, having trouble sleeping anyway. By morning I was a wreck, and it was going to be a busy day. I needed to let everyone know about the damage at the dock, meet with the surveyor from the insurance company, write a summary of events, meet with the lawyers, try to lift the arrest, make arrangements for hauling the boat and replacing the rudder, figure out why the engines weren't starting, and chase down the loan from John.

It was the end of October and the loan still wasn't in. It had been promised no later than October 15, and I needed it. Amber's mistakes and the rudder incident had made things considerably worse. The $150,000 would still be enough to pay everything, including $35,000 in interest due to lenders, but without it, I would be lost.

The marina already knew about the damage, but I had to notify my insurance company, my lawyers, and the admiralty marshal. The marshal, I learned, had not yet taken out the insurance policy. He hadn't gotten around to it. It had kind of slipped his mind. And according to my lawyers, it would be impossible to recover losses from the admiralty. They were a government agency, the main one for anything related to boats, so if they made a mistake, oh well. No one was going to enforce it against them. Same as when a government agency screws up in the United States.

This meant convincing either the marina or my insurance company to pay for a considerable amount of damage. As I sat in the plush offices of Isola & Isola, looking at legal texts on the shelves and the finely carved wood, I couldn't help yearning for a life with some dignity and stability. I had been Valedictorian and Most Likely to Succeed in high school, and I'd won every award possible at Stanford and had my pick of grad schools. I could have been a high-powered lawyer or anything else. We all say that in America, that anyone can grow up to be anything, and of course for 99 percent of the population it isn't true. But for me it had been, and I had squandered it.

The two lawyers who entered and sat opposite me were well groomed and expensive looking, while I sat in a T-shirt covered with stains from oil, diesel, paint, and rust. They were handsome and articulate. They had money and power, respect and important friends. They told me they would try to go after the marina, and all I could think of was what that would cost me in legal fees, and I had to ask about the fees, too, and express again that I was having a hard time financially, which was something I was tired of doing.

They read the summary of events I had written that morning for Pantaenius, my insurance company, including a description of the damage at the dock, and they told me again they would go after Queensway Quay, but I knew my only hope was to have this damage included in my own insurance claim, as part of the same event. The boat had been at the dock where the damage occurred because I'd had no choice of berthing because I had lost my rudder. It was all one sequence of events. But as I walked back to the boat to meet with the surveyor for Pantaenius, I wasn't convinced. They could call it two separate events, making me pay the $3,000 deductible twice, or even deny the entire claim.

I met Nancy on the boat, told her my thoughts, and she said, "Well, look at the bright side. It can always get worse." I couldn't even laugh.

The surveyor arrived, a friendly and handsome man in his fifties named Nick Bushnell. Very cheery in a button-down shirt, slacks, and a leather jacket. He was carrying a clipboard. I had done nothing wrong, but I was afraid anyway, as I suppose all people naturally are around insurance adjusters. I wondered whether I could be found negligent in some way that would invalidate my claim. I was afraid to tell him about the hydraulic ram coming loose, for instance. The ram coming loose was as simple as a loose screw, even if it was an enormous and specialized screw, and why hadn't it been checked and tightened before heading out to sea? If I was found to be negligent, I would lose the boat and much more. I couldn't possibly afford to pay for the tow or the salvage claim or the repairs.

"I know you've been through an awful time," Nick said. "But I just need to hear what happened and take note of the damage to the vessel."

I began with the sound of the rudder breaking off and told the story from there. I tried to help the insurance company by detailing how the German captain had lied and endangered the crew and vessel. Nick asked why I had abandoned ship, and I gave my reasons.

Nick listened carefully and took notes. "Sure," he said periodically. "What else could you do?" He sounded reassuring, and I hoped he was sincere.

He asked questions about each of the towing attempts, the tow back to Gibraltar, the kayak that was lost in the harbor, and the damage at the dock. "For now I want to make two lists," he said. "The damage that occurred before arriving at the dock and the damage that occurred afterward. That's really a shame the admiralty didn't act as they were required. You've had an awful bit of luck, mate. We'll see what we can do about that."

"I'm hoping it can be viewed as one event," I said. "So that I don't pay the deductible twice. It seems to me that it was the same event, since I'm here at this wall as a direct consequence of losing the rudder."

"Yes, I can see that. I can understand the argument, and I can try to put it to Pantaenius that way, in a favorable light, especially since it seems to me you've acted to the best of your ability throughout the ordeal to limit the damage. It's often the case that there's consequential damage after an event, and anything you've done to limit that argues in your favor, I would think."

I was pleased to hear this. He seemed to be taking my side.

"The one thing I'm still in the dark about," he said, "is how this rudder came off in the first place. You've said it was unskegged, and that certainly makes it weaker, but I have to believe they would have used the right sized post for it, and I'm not sure why that post would have sheared off. We'll see more once the boat comes out of the water, but can you tell me anything more about why it might have come off?"

This was the moment I had feared. I couldn't hold back the incident with the hydraulic ram any longer. "Well," I said. "I don't know why either, and I also want to see what it looks like out of the water, but I think it must have been a combination of factors. We were moving fast through high seas, about eleven knots with both engines at twenty-two hundred, and I think the seas were about twelve to fifteen feet at that point. I don't remember exactly."

"That's fine," Nick said. "I'll be looking up all the weather records. I have a friend at the RAF base here."

"Great," I said. "So I think it was the stress of that, combined with the lack of a skeg, and then the safety on the hydraulic ram failed, too, earlier in the night, and we had to put the emergency tiller on and reattach the ram, so it may have fatigued then, too."

"The hydraulic ram became detached from the rudder post?"

"Yes."

"Can we take a look at the ram?"

We went below and looked at the ram and the damage the fitting on the post had done to the wood. I felt sick. I was afraid this was going to invalidate the entire claim.

"Now how did that come off?" Nick asked.

"I don't know. It's not supposed to. That piece is supposed to lock."

"And how long was it off?"

"I don't know. Maybe ten minutes. It's hard to tell. It was kind of a panicked time."

"Yes, I can imagine. But you were able to get it back on in those seas. Did you hear any other sounds while you were doing that? Anything from the rudder?"

"It was banging a bit. I think its top edge must have hit against the hull, limiting how far it could swing. I imagine we'll see marks when we're hauled out."

So now I had confessed everything. I only hoped Nick and Pantaenius would be kind. Nick took some more notes, then had me turn the helm both ways while he watched the rudder post. He came back up to the pilothouse, made some more notes, told me he'd try "straight away" to arrange the lifting of the arrest and the haul out, then left.

Nancy and I heated some cans of soup for lunch and sat in the pilothouse staring into our bowls as we ate. The crew were helping to clean the mess from the tow, but they were also spending quite a bit of time on shore, which was fine. They were frequenting Dad's Bakehouse and the Clipper and other comfort spots. At the moment, it was getting windy and rainy, and that's always when food in a warm, homey pub sounds best.

After lunch, I tried again to start the engines. They wouldn't turn over, and by now their batteries were low. I was tired and didn't feel up to the project, but I decided to shop for a twelve-volt charger to give a direct boost to the start batteries. That would be a good backup to have on board anyway.

Nancy and I walked a long way in our foul-weather gear. Half the length of the country, in fact, to Sheppard's chandlery in Marina Bay. But we found what we needed, and the price wasn't marked up as high as usual. This was a rare find, perhaps even a mistake on their part. We snapped it up quickly and left.

I charged the starboard engine for quite a while, tried it with the boost and still didn't get it to turn over. So I went down to the engine room to inspect. No visible sign of problems on the starters, batteries, or connectors. I couldn't think of what else to check, so I just started checking everything, and when I looked at the oil in one of the engines, I found the problem. A terrible problem that I'd had before and hadn't thought was still possible. The oil was creamy, which meant salt water had gotten into the engines, siphoning back through the exhausts.

I was so frustrated I started yelling, which made Matt, Emi, and Nancy come down to the engine room. "The engines are full of salt water," I told them. "That's why they won't start."

"Oh no," Nancy said. "Not again."

"We have to drain the oil," I said, "then remove the injectors and blow the salt water out. Then we have to change the oil a million times and run under load at the dock with the fill caps off and our lines doubled, which we actually can't do because of the fouled props. Goddamnit."

I was demoralized during this time, pushing myself to get through each part of each day. Nancy encouraged me to remember the good parts of my last few years.

"Look at me," she said, and I looked up and she was beautiful and it was a comfort to have her with me. "You've changed people's lives. Think about Pete, and Dave, and others who care more about their writing now than anything else. Think about that guy who quit his job to go sailing, and the people who decided to retire early. Think of the great friends you have now that you met through the trips."

I couldn't help but smile. "Okay," I said. "Thanks."

"Seriously, David. It was a unique program you set up, and you worked hard, and this will all get better. And think of all the places we got to see, too."

"You're right," I said. "I'll quit moping." I did feel lucky and grateful to be with her.

I was helped also by Nick Bushnell. He managed to get the arrest lifted, and he convinced Pantaenius to accept the damage at the dock as part of the overall claim. He also found a yard in Spain that could haul us, in Sotogrande, about fifteen miles down the coast, inside the Mediterranean, and he arranged the tow to take us there. His help was an unexpected kindness.

Sotogrande has a lovely marina lined with pastel buildings. It's a large country club development, one of the exclusive golf and marina communities along the Costa Del Sol. Several tenders were waiting and helped the tug maneuver us to a stern tie along the inner quay. We couldn't go directly to the slip under the 150-ton travelift, unfortunately, because there was a waiting list to be hauled out. Nick Bushnell impressed upon me the need to visit the office several times each day to make sure I was hauled out soon. "You need to keep after the Spaniards a bit," he said.

Señor Guido, the yard manager, was likeable and mild-mannered, in his early forties and a bit plump. I explained my situation to him and he sympathized. My boat was also larger than any other sailboat the yard had ever hauled, if you considered its weight and beam, and it needed a lot of work done quickly, all covered by a large and reputable insurance company. This made it attractive business. And I was constantly in his office, just saying hello, so that none of the other captains could get around me. I was hauled out within three days, which Nick Bushnell said was a new record. If I could be repaired and back in the water within three weeks, I'd make the crossing to Mexico in time for all but the first charter.

When the boat was finally parked on the pavement, we could see the props bundled with dock line. Amazing they had still delivered enough power to maneuver up to the life raft. On most boats, attempting to use the props with line around them would have bent the shafts, but these were very thick.

The rudder was completely gone. Just an inch or so of steel rod sticking out from the bottom of the hull, its edges uneven from having been torn off. Nick Bushnell examined it and said there was no way of knowing exactly why it had done that. For the repair, the new rudder could be made in the yard, but the post, which would need to be solid Aquamet 22 or some other high-tech stainless steel, three and a half inches thick, would have to be custom-made in Algeciras or another city.

The challenge now was to get the repairs done on time. The shops in the yard were independent. They paid a commission to the marina, but I had to contract separately with the metal fabricators, the painters, the carpenters, etc. Each shop was busy, and the proprietors, each an oddball in his own way, had to be wooed.

The Spaniards have a peculiar workday. They arrive late, at about 9:30. Then they hit the local Café Ke for breakfast, which means coffee and almost an hour of shooting the breeze. Then they work from about 10:30 until 2:00. Then lunch from 2:00 until 4:00, then work again until 5:00, 6:00, or whenever they happen to feel like stopping. Every two or three days there's a national holiday and they don't work at all.

For the first couple of days, until I figured out this schedule, it was nearly impossible to find anyone. Endless walks back and forth across the yard, chasing shadows. When I finally caught on and appeared at Café Ke at 10:00 one morning, it was like a revelation. Absolutely everyone was there, all in one small room. In half an hour, I was able to circulate to everyone I needed.

My break from the daily antics of the boatyard was to drive to Puerto Banus with Nancy. Puerto Banus is one of the spots where the wealthiest people in the world gather. The harbor is tiny and filled with expensive yachts. The narrow, short road along this waterfront has become a car show. A Mercedes, Porsche, or BMW doesn't mean much here, except the rarest models. German practicality run over by the extravagant waste of British and Italian models. We saw Bentleys—not one but several—Aston Martins, Rolls Royces, Ferraris, and Lamborghinis. A few token Americans, such as the Shelby. We always enjoyed the show, and the fact that the drivers looked unconcerned, as if they weren't parading. We found the one or two reasonable places to eat, and after some food and a stroll, we'd hit the Internet café.

Two things were becoming clear. First, there was no way the boat would be finished in three weeks. It would be more like six weeks, probably, so I would lose all my crew. Second, I would have to fly to California for a week to put my business back together. Amber and her friend Heather, whom she had basically forced me to hire part-time, were messing up everything, and they were both about to bail for the big bucks at a dot-com, so I needed to hire and train someone new. The dot-com thing was annoying. Heather was straight out of a no-name college, with zero experience, and somebody was going to pay her $50,000 to start. I had made $27,000 as a lecturer teaching full-time at Stanford. Amber, who couldn't even pay bills correctly, was going to be a product manager and make even more.

MY SIX DAYS in California were extremely rushed. The first night back, I met with Amber and Heather.

Our office was just one room in a two-story building in Menlo Park, but it was big enough, and it was clean. Heather had done a lot of filing. She and Amber showed me what she had done, and it became clear that all she had done was filing, and I saw that she had filed documents related to my pickup truck in four different folders: "Nissan," "Truck," "David," and "Insurance." I had paid $1,000 or so over the past month for unnecessary and poorly executed filing.

Amber and Heather were both young. Amber about twenty-three, maybe, and Heather probably a year younger. They were acting like schoolgirls caught not having done their homework. It was odd. I was running a business. This was my life. It wasn't an amusement. But I could tell that less than complimentary comments about me had been the staple in this office for some time.

I was going through bills with Amber when we came across

one small one, for only $700, that had been paid late, after three written notices.

"I asked to have the small bills paid on time," I said. "Especially ones like this related to marketing materials."

"I know," Amber said. "I meant to pay this one, and he called several times. But I just forgot." Then she giggled. She actually giggled, and Heather, who was standing in the doorway, had to suppress a giggle. I learned a couple of years later that Amber was a stoner, so I have to assume now that this giggling was marijuana.

"Well it says here he's going to report me to credit agencies if it's not paid by September 1. But it looks like it wasn't paid until late October."

"Yeah, I guess that's what happened." And she smiled.

I looked at her, and I couldn't figure out how things had gotten this bad between us. "This is my credit," I said. "It's not funny."

"Look, David. You weren't here. I'm always having to juggle bills because you don't have enough money. I'm tired of it. Now you get to do the juggling."

"You mispaid bills by forty-eight thousand dollars in one month," I said. "And you let me be reported to credit agencies for small bills that we could have paid."

"Yeah, well, it's all done now. And it's late. We're outta here." She and Heather left.

I sat in my office under the fluorescent lights that night and finally just put my forehead down on the desk. I had been out of the country most of the time, but Amber was a smart, educated person, a Stanford graduate who had needed a job after her marriage engagement was broken off, and I was a reasonable and obviously trusting employer. I just didn't understand.

I spent every waking hour that week in the office. I went through all of our records and updated Quickbooks, having to call Amber several times a day because records were missing or entered incorrectly. She hadn't recorded deposits, for instance. I could find a deposit on a bank statement but had no way of knowing which three guest payments were included in it, and she had kept no record at all. Taxes were going to be a nightmare.

I also tried to save our winter charters. I made a lot of phone calls, but the list was too old. These were potential passengers from a month or two earlier who had never received a brochure in the mail or a follow-up call from Amber. By now, they had made other plans, booked other vacations. She had let my business die.

I wasn't convinced my new employee was going to be much better. If I'd had more time and other choices, I wouldn't have hired her. But I didn't have more time or other choices, and I had to have someone in the office. So I simplified our sales and customer service protocols, producing a series of sheets that told her exactly what to do at every step in all aspects of the business. The only important element I had to rely upon her for would be sales. I couldn't return calls from the middle of the ocean.

I still didn't have John's loan, and I needed it desperately, so I wanted to drive down to Hemet to see him, but he wouldn't return my calls, and I didn't know exactly where he was living. I had talked with him a week earlier, and he had told me then that he was delayed because the bank was slow to clear funds out of the trust. But he had assured me he was still giving the loan.

I did manage to pull in two more small loans, $5,000 and $10,000, but I was getting frantic. I was supposed to pay $35,000 in interest on December 1, a few days away, and I had no money.

I returned to Spain, trying to remain hopeful. But in just my one week away, the contractors had really slacked off, so I was in a panic trying to get everything done. My new crew were arriving in a few days and I planned to set sail in a week for Mexico. Everything had to be finished immediately.

So many things had to come together, it was overwhelming.

I really didn't think it could be finished on time. Further delay would mean canceling more winter charters, and possibly losing my crew again, neither of which I could afford.

The welders stayed until after 8 P.M. every day, and I had to pay overtime and tips and be there through all of it to pat their backs and do some of the work myself and keep them going.

The carpenter was high-maintenance, a young guy with long curly hair who felt he was an artist, but he did replace the deck piece and aft rail. The painters touched up the side of the boat and bow, and a few days before we were to launch, I actually had a new rudder and post in place. I still didn't have a skeg, but the fabricator assured me it would go quickly, and it did. He brought out some pieces of steel, welded them to the hull, welded the attachment, and there it was, ugly but burly. A rudder that looked a little small to me, smaller than the last one, but which certainly would never fall off. Nick Bushnell and the naval architect approved it for Pantaenius, so that I would still be insured, then some bottom paint was brushed on and we were ready.

My new crew had arrived a few days earlier and were working hard painting bilges and such. One of them was my friend Adriana, a Mexican lawyer I'd met at Stanford who was my partner on paper for the Mexican corporation. She was going to help me obtain permits for winter charters.

The last day was an ugly rush. The bill for the marina went higher than expected, the various contractors tacking on little bits here and there in outrageous ways, so Nick Bushnell was scrambling to get more money from the insurance company and I was scrambling to get enough of my own money to cover my part. I ran completely dry in my two checking accounts and on all of my credit cards and all of Nancy's cards. I finally had to borrow about $150 from my crew, otherwise the marina wasn't going to let us leave. The whole thing was embarrassing.

But we did leave, and right away, the steering felt wrong. Just coming out of the travelift and crossing the marina, I was having trouble going straight. Even allowing for greater lag time in the steering, it wasn't consistent. It felt random. I desperately wanted to hide the problem from Nick, so that my insurance would remain intact, but he could tell. Once we had cleared the channel and were on our way to Gibraltar to pick up the new anchor chain, he tried the helm.

"It does seem to be a problem," he said. "You can probably manage it, but if you wanted to go back, I could try to present that to Pantaenius."

"I'm screwed financially if I don't keep going," I said. "I can't afford new crew or to cancel my winter charters."

Nick raised his eyebrows and shrugged. He was my friend. He was doing everything possible to get me to Mexico where I could bring in some income. That was my highest priority, to bring in some money to pay my bills.

I kept testing the steering and decided we could make it to Mexico. It wasn't a safety or seaworthiness issue. It was just a convenience issue. It was difficult to steer. I had to stay right on top of it, and even then, I sometimes couldn't keep it straight. The crew would be frustrated, and our crossing time would be slow, probably six weeks, but the rudder would stay on, and we'd get used to it.

"I think I need to continue on," I told Nick. My crew was listening, and they looked worried, but they weren't saying anything. I had never wanted to reach this point, where I was forced to go to sea. I believed a captain should take a boat to sea only when he felt it was ready. But that would have meant giving up on the business and screwing all of my lenders and Stanford Continuing Studies and teachers and students. I had made a lot of promises.

We rounded Gibraltar, into the bay, then I had to turn ninety degrees to starboard to enter the channel for the marinas. It was hard to get the turn to begin, then I swung too far to starboard, then tried not to overcorrect, but it wasn't turning back at all. We were heading for the rocks. So I turned farther to port, and then we swung too far in that direction. We swung four or five times before straightening out, as if I had never driven a boat before in my life.

By the time we were done taking on our 450 feet of chain, it was after dark, and I decided it was stupid for us to sail for Mexico without a good night's sleep. The crew appreciated dinner ashore, and we all turned in early.

We left just after daylight. The crew tried hard to steer straight, but it was close to impossible. The rudder seemed to have a mind of its own, with no pattern at all. They were good crew, but they had to say something.

"It's inconvenient," I said in response. "But it's not a safety or seaworthiness issue." This was Gibraltar to Cancún, almost six thousand miles on the track through St. Lucia, a trip that would take at least six weeks, sailing twenty-four hours a day. They were dreading the experience, and I couldn't blame them. But I didn't feel I had a choice.

Then, about an hour and a half into the trip, we heard a terrible grinding sound from one of the engines and it lost power. I took the helm, yanked the throttles back to neutral, and went below.

Nothing was visible on the engine, and all its gauges and fluids checked out normal. I had a crew member at the helm run the engine at different revs, and the sound happened again at high revs, but I couldn't tell where it was coming from. The engine bucked when it made the sound and was clearly under enormous strain. It could have been a bent shaft, but both shafts were turning smoothly. It could have been the starter engaging for some reason, but that seemed unlikely. It could have been something deep in the guts, I supposed, a piston somehow sticking or rusted bearings around the bases of the rods, but I didn't know that part of the engine. It could have been something wrong with the transmission. I checked the transmission oil, but we were getting bounced in seas, and it was difficult to see much. The dipstick was scalding and had to be unscrewed with an 18 mm socket, then pried out with two fingers, but in the quick look I was able to take, it looked fine.

I went back on deck and took over the helm. "We only need one engine," I said. "Even if we can't figure out the problem with the port engine, we can still make it on the starboard. We were going to run on one engine most of the time anyway, to save diesel, and of course we'll try to sail as much as possible. And we can have the port engine checked out when we're in the Canaries. But I realize this sucks, and the steering sucks. I just need to think about it for a few minutes."

I gave the helm to someone else and went back to sit on the poop deck with Nancy.

It was sunny and the wind and waves weren't bad. It seemed like we could just go, and we'd make it. We had all our food, and one engine, at least, and the crew would be all right.

"I want to keep going," I said. "But I think it would be a stupid decision. We should have both engines, and we should know what the problem is, and the steering is awful. It will be so frustrating, the crew will probably get off at the next port, in the Canaries. And then we'll be stuck in the Canaries, with no cash and no crew and the insurance probably unwilling to cover the problems. The truth is, even if the steering and engine were fine, I don't have any money for diesel along the way or to pay the crew when we arrive. I'm screwed. John's loan just hasn't come in on time."

Nancy didn't say anything. She looked unhappy.

"I'm sorry," I said. "I'll tell the crew we're turning around. The worst would be if we got caught in a storm with steering that wasn't right and we lost control of the boat. That would be worse, I guess."

"This is bad enough, though," Nancy said. "You'll have to cancel classes, and hire new crew, and you won't be able to pay the interest you owe. . . . It goes on and on."

"I know."

"What a nightmare," she said.

So we turned around, running on one engine. I radioed the marina in advance and let them know I had one engine and a new rudder that wasn't steering correctly, so they gave me an easy outside slip.

After docking, I called Nick Bushnell and went looking for Fred the Perkins dealer, but Fred had just left for New Zealand. As my crew waited around for the next two days and did some work repainting bilges, I tried my best to get a quick repair. Fred's mechanic and the mechanics from Sheppard's and another mechanic all looked at it, but the engine wouldn't repeat its problem. We ran it hard at the dock, in gear, with triple dock lines, but we couldn't get it to make the sound. We did a compression test, which turned out normal. Everything else checked out normal, too. The engine problem remained mysterious, as did the rudder problem.

These problems were nothing, however, compared to my financial problems. I was calling John several times a day, leaving messages on his answering machine that, by the end, were basically pleading. I told him I was going to go under if I didn't get the loan. I suggested giving the loan in stages, or even just giving a smaller loan.

I was at the Internet café for long stretches each evening, and under advice from Rand, my principal lender, I had sent an e-mail to all of the lenders asking for a restructuring of the loans. I told them that with the setbacks from the war in Kosovo, construction that was delayed and had gone over budget, repairs from the loss of the paint and the rudder, loss of crew, and a promised loan that had not yet materialized, I wasn't able to pay the first interest payments that were now a week overdue. I had offered an interest rate that was too high and a payback schedule that was too quick if anything went wrong. I now needed $87,000 within the next week, at a minimum, to prevent American Express from taking legal action against me. And I had other bills. I was asking the lenders for a restructuring of the loans at a lower interest rate over a longer period of time, and I was asking for new loans to cover my bills now to keep the business afloat.

It was an unpleasant letter for the lenders to receive. They wanted more info, which I gave, and Rand gave me $24,000. We had previously agreed that, because he and Lee planned to use a lot of charter time on the boat, they would pay $1,000 per month toward operating expenses over a two-year period, so he was accelerating all of those payments into one lump sum. It was remarkably generous. But none of the other lenders seemed likely to give or loan more money. As several of them put it very clearly, they didn't want to risk throwing good money after bad.

I finally received a short e-mail from John, titled "Nut-Vice Judas." He had praised me on previous occasions for running a unique and risky business, for "putting my nuts in the vice" to make my dreams happen. In this e-mail, he said he couldn't give me a new loan because of various bills and such. It was difficult to believe, however, that $3.5 million had evaporated in a few weeks, so that less than $150,000 was left. Amber must have told him not to give me the loan. That was the only explanation Nancy or I could believe.

These were grueling, shameful times. Rand suggested bankruptcy. I took offense, at first. Bankruptcy seemed unimaginable. But when no new loans came in, and Rand canceled his $24,000 check to cut his losses, which bounced a lot of checks and left my Citibank account $11,000 overdrawn, and *Grendel* still didn't sell, even at a reduced price, and my new employee wasn't selling any new trips, and I couldn't even get my engine fixed, I had to admit, finally, that I had failed. I took late-night walks around Gibraltar, the streets empty and hollow, what was happening to my business and life shielded by disbelief. I had liked who I was—the founder, teacher, and captain for these educational charters. A man with exquisite, self-made freedom. Now I was someone else, someone who had failed and was going to cheat a lot of people out of their money, plain and simple. A guy who didn't pay his debts, a man with no integrity. I told Rand and my new employee that I was going to have to put the boat up for sale here in Gibraltar and probably file for bankruptcy, unless it sold right away for a high amount. I would write a note to the lenders explaining.

But my new employee jumped the gun. She told all of the lenders and passengers right away that I had filed for bankruptcy. She even put it on our answering machine message. Just the fact that I was considering it was supposed to be confidential, and this was outrageous. I was very angry.

One of the lenders sent me a note that she had been considering lending more money, a significant amount of money, and she was amazed and upset to learn from our answering machine that I had already filed for bankruptcy. I responded to this and other long e-mails with my own long e-mails trying to explain, but the damage had been done. I had failed in the business. I didn't want anyone to throw away more money. On top of this, my new employee had handled the situation in the worst possible way. I hated every minute of trying to deal with this mess. I really wanted to die.

I sent the crew home, buying their tickets and paying the marina bill with the last money I had. I could leave the boat cleared of expenses, but that was it. I didn't have enough money left over even for my own plane ticket home. I had poured everything into the business.

I arranged with Nick to bring the boat back to Sotogrande, where the insurance might be willing to pay for repair of the engine and hauling of the boat to modify the rudder. Or they might not. In any case, the marina there would cost less per day than Gibraltar, and the boat would be more likely to sell, and the repairs might get done. It was the best I could do for the lenders. If they wanted me to return in January to work on the boat, to fix it up for sale, I would do that too.

Rand paid for my flight home, and Nancy's parents paid for hers. On the morning of the day we were to fly out, we moved the boat from Gibraltar to Sotogrande with two crew Nick had lined up for us. We paid them with the food from our refrigerators and freezers.

It was a sad last trip on the boat. It had been such a grueling, pointless struggle: getting through construction and financing and launch in Turkey; then the charters with the various problems, including water in the engines and paint falling off and the emergency haul-out; then the quick trip across the Med, the rudder falling off, and ten hours at the helm for the towing attempts, followed by six frustrating weeks in the yard, trying to get the Spaniards to do the work, afraid all the time of the bills I couldn't pay; and now these new problems with one of the engines and the new rudder, with bankruptcy as the whipped cream and cherry. I'd had enough.

AFTER PAYING FOR my flight home, Rand set up an appointment with a bankruptcy attorney, and he gave me cash to get through the next few weeks. If he hadn't done this, I don't know how I would have gotten by. I didn't have even $10, cash or credit.

This bankruptcy attorney gave us some helpful information, but he was not up to the task of a complicated bankruptcy. I soon met with another attorney, recommended by another of my lenders, and he seemed capable. After a lot of discussion, I decided to file a personal bankruptcy under Chapter 7, with the three corporations (California, Gibraltar, and Mexico) listed as personal assets. I didn't have the option of reorganization, because my debts, both secured and unsecured, were too large.

Bankruptcy law is very generous to the debtor. I might be allowed to keep *Grendel,* for instance, my forty-eight-foot boat that still hadn't sold. I could claim a $50,000 homeowner's exemption, and this, combined with the $34,000 bank mortgage and $10,000 in private loans secured against it, meant that the bankruptcy trustee could not make any money from selling it, so he most likely would consider it not worth the effort.

In the end, I hoped that most of my lenders would be repaid from the sale of the boat in Spain, and I would keep *Grendel* (with its mortgages still intact). I would still have other private debts, however, which the court would discharge but which I would have to repay anyway. I owed my mother $60,000, for instance, and my sister $11,000. I would also need to repay money that I was borrowing from Rand to get through the bankruptcy and to get my life back together. I would end up at far less than zero net worth.

And then I ran into new problems. I called the attorney general of California's office because I was not able to refund passenger deposits for the winter charters. I had collected a measly $14,371 in deposits, from six passengers, but I had no cash to repay even this amount. I had a California Seller of Travel license, however, and I had contributed yearly to the Travel Consumer Restitution Fund as a part of this ongoing licensing process. I thought my passengers might be able to make claims against this fund to get their money back, and I wanted to make sure they received their money, so I was calling on their behalf to find out how and where they should make their claims.

After several voicemail messages back and forth, I spoke over the phone with a deputy attorney general who told me very directly that he was going to come after me. He said that every time I had used passenger deposits to pay for diesel, crew, slip fees, food, or any other operating expense, I had committed embezzlement, a felony offense.

He claimed this on the basis that I had two corporations, one in California and one in Gibraltar. The California corporation had a Seller of Travel license, had collected the monies, and, in his opinion, was a Seller of Travel and not a "carrier." The Gibraltar corporation owned the boat and was therefore the carrier. A carrier can legally use deposits to pay for a boat's operating expenses, whereas a Seller of Travel cannot.

I realized at this point that I had made a mistake. I should not have called, and my passengers had no right to make claims against the fund. I had the Seller of Travel license only for when I leased boats, but in this case I had not leased a boat. I had used my own boat and was a "carrier," like a cruise line, rather than a Seller of Travel, which is basically a travel agent.

I tried to explain this to the deputy, calmly. The Gibraltar corporation was owned by the California corporation and had been set up only to allow flagging of the vessel. It had no bank account, no employees, no income or expenses, and no office. The California corporation could not have used the passenger deposits to buy the trips from the Gibraltar corporation, because there was no one to pay, and the Gibraltar corporation could not have paid for operating expenses because it had no bank account or employees. In summary, the California company was the "carrier," I had not broken any laws, and my passengers had no right to make claims against the fund. I apologized for making this mistake.

The deputy attorney general said no. Just said no, flying in the face of common sense and reason. It was hard to know how to respond. He understood what I was saying, but he still claimed that the company with no bank account and no employees was the company I had to pay for obtaining the charters, and that if I had ever paid operating expenses with money from the California company, it was a felony charge of embezzlement and I was going to jail.

It was just before Christmas, sunny and bright outside. I was trying to think of some other simpler way of explaining this to him. Surely a deputy attorney general of California was capable of basic reason. I was getting scared. Then he told me the only thing I could do that would keep him from pressing charges would be to repay in full the $14,371 I owed to passengers. I explained that I had no money at all, that everything had gone

into the business, because I had in fact not embezzled anything, not even my own savings and wages from teaching, and
this was why I had to file for bankruptcy. But he said I had to
pay or he would press charges.

I made my mistake with him then. I didn't raise my voice,
and I didn't get angry. I just asked, in a very humble tone,
what happened if I contested this, because it didn't make
sense. I felt I was allowed at least the question, to find out
what my options were, but this was a mistake.

I began calling attorneys immediately. I also called one of my
lenders, who happened to be a deputy attorney general of California in a different office. He thought the charges were nuts,
but it was clear he wasn't going to step into the case and inter-
fere, either. Apparently it was bad etiquette for one deputy to
step in and question another deputy's case. So I found an
attorney, a guy named Jack, who specialized in this area and
had in fact written part of the current Seller of Travel Law. He
represented cruise lines and travel agents. And he knew this
deputy personally.

Jack met with me on Christmas Eve. Rand was lending me
the money to pay his fees. Jack said this deputy was known as
a hothead and it was too bad I had questioned his authority,
even obliquely. He would take it personally and make sure he
nailed me, even if it was a waste of time and not in the best
interests of the citizens of California. On the very day I had
spoken with the deputy, Jack had put a case on his desk
involving about $150,000 in real fraud. A company had sold a
lot of trips to Baja California with no intention of ever providing the trips. After they collected the deposits from consumers, they packed up and left town. The consumers filed
police reports. Jack presented the case for prosecution, and
the deputy decided not to take it. He took mine instead.

This, Jack said, was to make his numbers look good. He
could win the case against me easily. I had called the AG's
office myself, basically turning myself in, and although the

case against me had zero merit and was a departure from the AG office's own practice of "following the money" to determine who the carrier was, the deputy knew that I was declaring bankruptcy and didn't have any money. This meant I wouldn't be able to pay the $20,000–$25,000 to defend myself in court. He would have an auditor review my books, and he would file hundreds of counts of felony embezzlement against me, for every time I had paid an expense to run a charter. Fighting this would be too expensive and high-risk for me, since if a jury didn't understand the case I could end up in jail.

I was speechless when I first heard all of this. This deputy attorney general was letting $150,000 in real fraud slip by and coming after me instead, on the basis of an idea that didn't follow even his own practices. And he could get away with it because I was poor.

Jack dictated a letter to him that day, explaining everything and asking him to drop the case. Jack also used the occasion to further some of his own interests, adding a garbled paragraph about the history of Seller of Travel Law. The inclusion of these vague bureaucratic threats, combined with the fact that Jack had trouble arguing my case clearly (I had to revise many of his sentences to make them understandable), did not inspire confidence. By the end of the day, I realized Jack was a hack. I was capable of making the case more clearly. But of course I didn't have the personal relationship with the deputy, and I wasn't a celebrated lawyer or one of the authors of the Seller of Travel Law. I had to take what I could get.

There was another issue we discussed that day, which was my consumer bond. The Travel Consumer Restitution Fund was really a secondary fund. My primary protection was a $10,000 bond through Redland Insurance Company. When I contacted Redland to find out how my passengers could make their claims, Redland responded by immediately canceling my bond and hiring a collection agency to beat the shit out of me.

They refused the claim and also sued me for $12,000 to indemnify them against claims.

So Jack dictated a letter to these folks, too. The California attorney general and Redland Insurance Company were making my bankruptcy and the loss of my business seem like the easy parts. The only silver lining was that I had fallen about as low as I could fall, including feelings of fear, guilt, shame, self-pity, and persecution, and still I had no interest in putting a gun to my head. Apparently I wasn't going to follow in my father's footsteps and kill myself. So that was good news.

After this meeting, I asked Rand for a loan for the $14,371. I didn't want to spend my life in prison on several hundred bogus felony counts, and I didn't have the money to fight the charges.

Rand had already done more than pay my flight home. He had also given me some cash to get through the end of December, set up the appointment with the bankruptcy attorney, and even given me a job. A few weeks before, when I had still been in Gibraltar, he had told me he wanted to set up a Web site that would review and rank crewed charter companies—a consumer guide for vacations on the water. He said he would hire me for a year to travel the world, interview charter companies, evaluate their services, and write the reviews. It was incredibly generous, and the thought of it helped me get through a hard time. But he wasn't going to loan me this new money, even as an advance against my pay. He didn't want his loans to be never-ending.

So Christmas was not very merry. Everyone knew I was about to file for bankruptcy, and I had no credit whatsoever, and I needed to find a $14,371 loan.

It's hard to get people to loan you money right before you file a bankruptcy that will discharge that loan. Who on earth would do it? But what kept me trying was this thought: Could a jury of ordinary folks be counted on to understand that the Gibraltar company was set up only to register the vessel? Wouldn't it be pretty easy to paint a picture that I was doing something dirty in setting up these foreign corporations? Most Americans instinctively distrust that kind of thing.

Then Rand relented and said he would loan $10,000 if I could get the $4,371 from someone else. It was to be an advance against the Redland Insurance bond, for a few weeks. Rand and his wife, Lee, were saving me again, and I was unspeakably grateful, but I still needed the other part of the loan.

For the next two weeks, as I filled out my bankruptcy schedules, tried to clean up nearly impossible taxes after Amber's lack of accounting, and worked on a business plan for Rand, I tried to find a loan, but there weren't many places to turn. Finally, I called Charlotte Calhoun, my last hope.

Charlotte Calhoun was the custodian for a very large fund that gave gifts to various causes. She didn't owe me anything, and there was no compelling reason for her to give me a loan. She was in her early sixties, I think, and had been a student in one of my Continuing Studies courses in creative nonfiction. Her memoir, which took place in China and was set against the background of her husband's long illness and eventual death, was beautifully written and moving. I had encouraged her, and I had offered to keep looking at her manuscript after the course ended. She had also come on a charter in Turkey in the summer of 1998; afterward she set up a yearly $10,000 gift to Stanford Continuing Studies to be used to pay the salaries of visiting teachers on my trips. I had never asked her for a loan for the new boat, because I knew she would not be interested in that kind of thing and I hadn't wanted to offend her. But I called her now, and I told her the situation.

Charlotte said yes. I felt terrible asking her, but she was extremely gracious about it. She wanted to loan the full $14,371, in case the bond never came through, and she wasn't worried about repayment. I could repay her if it became convenient. She thought keeping me out of jail on trumped-up charges was worth the money.

I was so grateful, I cried. None of the events of the past

months had made me cry. But kindness—generosity that isn't obligated in any way—is much more affecting.

Charlotte's loan saved me. The money was put into a trust account with Jack, and the deputy called off his auditor in San Francisco. The deputy also sent a letter saying the AG's office wouldn't take action against me as long as the money went to all the passengers and I didn't break the law. This last clause allowed him to still come after me at any time on the same bogus charges, which was his way of keeping me quiet. Jack was supposed to get an admission that the charges were inappropriate, but he failed.

I had to give up on the $10,000 bond from Redland Insurance Company, also. The deputy had promised to go after Redland for the bond money, since by law they should have had to pay, but of course he didn't follow through. They were still suing me for $12,000, however, to indemnify the bond amount and to pay their collection agency. They put marks on my credit history and threatened me in every way they could. So I just listed them in my bankruptcy papers and gave up.

By this time, toward the end of January 2000, the business idea with Rand had become more than just an online consumer guide to yacht charters. We had decided to go for a full boating portal. There was no good boating portal on the web yet, and vertical portals, which focused on bringing together vendors and consumers for a particular industry, were the hottest item for new venture capital investment. Rand's brother-in-law, Tom, was a venture capitalist and CEO of a start-up, formerly the CFO of Safeway and other large corporations, and he was willing to help us out. I was writing a business plan, and he was going to review it and help us through revisions and research until we were ready to present our plan for funding. Rand, in his characteristic generosity, was willing to split the founder's shares with me, fifty-fifty.

I clung to this opportunity. This was before tech stocks

crashed, and the opportunity looked very good, especially compared with anything else in my life. I put the plan together by the end of January, after about three weeks of working around the clock, and it was a good first stab. Rand's brother-in-law Tom was impressed. The total market was over $50 billion, the magic number, and the industry was fragmented, with tens of thousands of small businesses and great inefficiencies. It was a perfect example of a market in which a portal could gain dominance, both on the business-to-consumer and business-to-business sides. My plan was for an infomediary, a business that would consolidate information and facilitate transactions, trying to capture only a tiny percentage of a huge volume.

I worked long hours polishing this plan for presentation to investors. Timing was everything. If we were too late, we'd get nothing. And then, on February 8, 2000, the new issue of *Boating Industry International* featured an article on Internet portals for the boating industry. They had surveyed the field, doing exactly the research I had done, and much of my business plan was in that article. They confirmed that all of the current companies approaching the opportunity were falling short. But the article also listed some new sites that were about to go up, and one of these presented a problem. When I went to their site, which hadn't been up two weeks earlier, I read about their management team and funding. They were six months ahead of us, and that meant we were sunk.

I asked Tom about other options, about where I could go next, and he suggested approaching them for a partnership. Since the Internet game was a race, in which companies could not develop quickly enough no matter how fast they moved, we might take care of some aspect of the portal in cooperation with them.

So I called the CEO of this dot-com, and he was interested, but he was going to be out of the country for a few weeks. We would meet when he returned. This delay was not good, because Rand was going to throw in the towel, on my recommendation, and things were moving so fast in the industry that even three weeks later, our position was no longer quite as strong. So I kept the appointment but turned it into a job interview.

I was hired, and Nancy took a job at carclub.com, just a few blocks away along the waterfront in San Francisco. We were both happy defectors from teaching, working crazy hours but feeling like it was going to amount to something.

The bankruptcy went well, also. I filed, had my hearing, then needed to wait three months to find out if any of the creditors would file objections to the discharge. It didn't look like anyone was going to do that. My private lenders were remarkably gracious about the whole thing, telling me they had made the investment with their eyes open, knowing it was a risky business. Only Amber was nasty about it, which was absurd, since she was the only person other than me who could be considered responsible for the failure. She and Heather were trying to sue me through the Employment Development Department, and Nancy and I received a lot of e-mails and phone calls from Amber, but none of this had any effect.

At the bankruptcy hearing, I was questioned for about forty-five minutes, compared to the usual five, because my case was unusual and a bit complicated. But I had nothing to hide, and I even entertained the crowd. *Oohs* and *aahs* as they heard about each new disaster in the business. The captain who had dumped *Grendel* near Guatemala, the rudder incident off Casablanca. It was certainly a story no one had heard before, and obviously I had done everything in my power to prevent the eventual failure. It still felt awful, though, to be in court skipping out on my debts. Bankruptcy may be legal, but it doesn't feel right. I was just hoping the dot-com would succeed and I'd be able to pay everyone back.

The dot-com did well at first. We received a much larger

round of funding, and no one believed that the stock crash that began in April 2000 would continue for very long. Everyone expected recovery within a year or less, including the venture capitalists. In hindsight, this was silly, but it was what people in the dot-com world, including me, believed.

Our dot-com was more traditional than most, since our industry—boating—was conservative. We had older managers and dressed at least business casual, and we didn't have a foosball table or any other games or wild parties. We just worked eighty-hour weeks for five months straight to launch the site. And I found my way to advance within the company.

Though I was hired in business development, I became the "contract guy," and everyone had me review legal agreements before negotiation or signing. I was interested in contracts because they revealed that business is based, finally, on nothing more than trust and hope, despite what we otherwise believe. What holds the business world together is a house of cards. We didn't have an in-house legal department, and I was one of only a few people in the sixty-five-person company who could read carefully. So I began reporting directly to every member of our executive management.

Near the end of the summer, I was finally promoted to work directly under the CFO. I would be responsible for all legal agreements for the company and its subsidiaries. I would call one of our several law firms when I had questions, but I would do as much of the work myself as possible, to minimize our legal fees, since by this time the company was trying to reduce expenses in a difficult market. My change in position was announced at a company-wide meeting after my work was praised, and I was happy until I found out they wanted me to take on these greater responsibilities without giving me anything in return. They weren't promoting me to director level, just changing my title to manager of contracts and business development, and they weren't offering more pay or more stock options.

I stuck up for myself, and the CFO was condescending to

me. He was a good boss, generally, but now he told me I needed to walk before I learned to run. I hated the clichés of business. Thinking in business is extremely lazy. If I hadn't needed the job to repay my mother and Rand and all my other creditors, I would have given him an ultimatum, but instead I settled for additional stock options and the promise that I would advance in rank and salary soon, most likely in a couple of months, after my formal review.

So I went to work even more determined to show I deserved to be raised up. I tackled a company we had aquired. Within three weeks, and after one visit up to their offices in Seattle, I showed they had more than five hundred clients not under contract, legal notices on their Web site that were meaningless, since they had never incorporated and weren't a legal entity, and no protocols for who would review or execute contracts. They were also breaking the law every day by copying material from other Web sites and encouraging their clients to do the same. It was an intellectual property nightmare, and an extreme example of mismanagement and lack of due diligence. The general manager did not understand even the basics of business law. As I pointed out the problems to him, he had difficulty understanding, and he took no responsibility.

I reported back to the CFO and he said go get 'em. With help from our law firm, I rewrote all of the company's contracts and legal notices and instituted due diligence. I reviewed the original acquisition of the company and followed up on licensing and stock issues. By the time I was through, I had greatly reduced our liability and put through an enormous volume of legal work while at the same time reducing our monthly legal bills from $45,000 to $8,000. In my final report, though, our president asked that I soften my exposure of the general manager's culpability. I was basically forced to do this. Instead of telling me by e-mail, which was our usual way of operating in the company, he came down and sat with me personally. He made it clear that if I didn't soften my exposure of negligence, I might lose my job. I gathered that some of the lack of due diligence in the original acquisition of the company might have been his own fault.

So I had to change my report, and I moved on. In addition to my work with our subsidiary, I wrote every new contract the dot-com needed for various vendors, contractors, and employees. I reviewed, revised, and negotiated contracts that came in from our largest partners, from development contracts to eBay. I substituted for in-house legal, negotiating directly even with the infamous AOL. I also wrote, reviewed, and negotiated European contracts for our new European office.

At my review, I argued again that I should be promoted to the director level and given a raise. But the CFO kept putting me off. He did this by never getting around to finishing my review. These were hard times in the dot-com world, with stock prices falling ever lower, and he needed to bring in another round of funding. He was failing at this, and all of his other duties were being put on the back burner. The truth, though, is that he didn't stick up for me. I had a lot of inside information on that company, so I knew that a few other people were getting raises because their executives were putting in a pitch for them. At these same meetings, my boss was not putting in a pitch for me. Instead, he was just relying on me to cover more and more of his work as he focused on getting new investment.

In December, we had massive layoffs and I couldn't help but think that many good people were losing their jobs because of mismanagement by our executives. They had paid a ludicrous amount for our subsidiary, our chief strategy officer was a nincompoop who had spent hundreds of thousands on content we weren't even using, the general manager who should have been fired was promoted instead, and the company building our Web site was using kids straight out of college who billed us at more than $200 per hour. These were the excesses that brought dot-coms down. The CEO of Scient, the company building our Web site, was reportedly making $100 million a year. I hated seeing good people lose their jobs because of these excesses.

I kept my job because I was saving the company almost $40,000 a month in legal fees, plus doing much of the executive management team's work and running the Product Store, and I was being paid only a little more than $5,000 per month. Our CEO pretended he was in a similar situation, since he wasn't being paid a salary, but at the same time he was scooping up entire percentage points of stock in the company, 2 percent here, 2 percent there, striking deals influenced by his position as chairman of the board and by the fact that his wife was a partner in one of the two large venture capital firms that were funding us.

I grew to truly dislike our CEO. Usually, when things are going wrong for a large group, you can't point the finger at just a few people, but with our CEO, president, general manager, and chief strategy officer, it was not rocket science to figure out what went wrong.

The bankruptcy court had listed the boat in Spain for seven or eight months now, but it hadn't sold. This wasn't a surprise, really. I had told my lenders the boat would sell only if it was fixed up, with a fresh coat of varnish and a thorough cleaning, inside and out. No one buys a boat that hasn't been maintained. I had offered to do this work for free if they paid for flights and materials, but the lenders didn't want to spend more money. By now, the varnish would be gone, the wood warping, the galvanized rigging rusted, and there might even be corrosion inside the hull.

In mid-November, the bankruptcy trustee made a final offer to the secured creditors, an offer that was not at all in their best interests, since the role of any bankruptcy trustee is to protect unsecured creditors (those whose loans haven't been registered as liens against the vessel). The trustee also indicated that if the secured creditors did not agree to this plan, he might just close the case and abandon the asset back to me, the debtor. So my secured creditors asked the trustee to close the case as soon as possible. Once the boat was abandoned back to me, they would still have their liens, and the unsecured creditors would be gone.

I began work right away on a new deal with my secured creditors. In return for a much lower interest rate (the minimum federal applicable rate instead of 15 percent) and much longer term (six years instead of three, with the first two years deferred), I would repay the full principle plus interest calculated at the new rate, and give charter time, and invest all of the money needed to put the boat back into service.

I tried not to rush into this. I tried to stop and think about what I was doing. I didn't have to go back into business, after all. I didn't have to put myself at risk again. I didn't want to wreck Nancy's life, either. But even when I would pause and try to think, it seemed that the decision had already been made. My mind would just stop, unable to go any further. Perhaps this was the unconscious control my father's death still had over me. Or perhaps I would have been tied to the sea even without his death. But I also couldn't let my private lenders take a loss. And I wanted the boat and that life back again. That life, unlike this one at the dot-com, had been self-determined. It had meant something.

My plan was to charter in the Virgin Islands and nowhere else. Once I fixed up the boat and sailed across the Atlantic I would simplify and streamline the business. No more complicated licenses and permits in sketchy third-world countries, no office in California, no permanent employees, and no educational charters. I would charter only through brokers, who sell the boat for a week and do all of the sales and follow-up with their clients. For the first two years I would make no payments on the loans, and for the next four years I would be paying on only $185,000 in loans at the lowest legal interest rate, since Rand and Lee had agreed, in their characteristic generosity, to have their $250,000 loan paid after the other loans, beginning in six years and ending at ten years. It was a very attractive plan, a rare second chance.

The difficult part was coming up with $100,000 to put the boat back into service. I owed $20,000 to the marina in Spain and would need to pay tens of thousands for legal fees, a new insurance policy, a new paint job, new standing rigging, new varnish, equipment overhauls, a new dinghy and outboard, etc. It was a solid hull, made of the highest-grade steel and only two years old, but all the cosmetics would have to be redone. The dot-com had promised a bonus, and I needed to make sure I received it. I also needed to sell *Grendel*. Nancy and I began working on *Grendel* immediately, at the end of November, to have it ready for sale when the bankruptcy trustee officially closed my case. Nancy would also take out credit cards to help fund the new business.

At the dot-com, I was switching my focus. They were still jerking me around about my bonus and a promotion and raise. They had been promising all three since late July, and now it was December and my boss, the CFO, was fired along with much of the rest of the company. He was going to stay for another month, to finish a few things and because new investment is less likely if the CFO has just left, but then he'd be gone and I'd have even less chance of getting the bonus or anything else.

The entire dot-com era was an anomaly for employees. Because of stock options, employees for one of the few very narrow windows in history were able to get back more than they put in. But that was over now. Stock prices were down, and companies were treating employees with no regard whatsoever.

On the weekends, instead of working for the company, I was fixing up *Grendel* for sale. When I finally listed it in January 2001, a bad time of year in a worse economy, a flood of buyers came to look at it right away. I was offering a solid boat at a reasonable price. On Saturday of the first weekend, Michael and Eva Pardee came to look at it, and they fell in love. Two days later, they put in an offer for the full asking price. Michael was also interested in what I was doing with the ninety-foot boat. He volunteered to spend a month in Spain helping me get the boat ready, and to crew across the Atlantic.

Everything was going well. In addition to selling *Grendel* and setting up a new company in Gibraltar, called Bird of Paradise Yacht Charters Limited, I had signed on with a clearinghouse that would hold our charter calendar for brokers, and I had found a broker who would sell trips on our boat before seeing it. This was unusual. Most brokers wait until they've seen a boat at one of the boat shows before they'll book it, and we wouldn't be at the shows until November. This broker sold our two holiday charters—Christmas and New Year's—right away, at $21,500 for each week. He was an eccentric South African in Florida, with a grand way of speaking, and though our initial negotiations were contentious—he wanted to be our clearinghouse as well as our broker, and he wanted a 20 percent commission on trips instead of the usual 15 percent— I was firm and he finally relented. On each of these $21,500 weeks, after broker commission and the clearinghouse and operating expenses, we would net more than $15,000.

I used a lot of my time at work to arrange repairs for the boat, which I renamed *Bird of Paradise*. First I would need to fix the mysterious problems with the port engine and steering. I talked with Nick Bushnell, the surveyor in Gibraltar, fairly often now, trying to get the boat hauled out and repaired before I arrived. But the engine did not get looked at, and when the time finally came for the yard at Sotogrande to haul the boat, after a delay because their travelift needed repair, they tried but gave up. They said my boat was too heavy. Their lift had been de-rated during the repairs and wasn't strong enough now. They had tried, and they weren't going to try again.

Even though there were some frustrations, I was generally

happy making these arrangements for the boat; I was grateful to have a second chance. It was also a happy time because I was thinking about marriage with Nancy. We were partners moving into a good future together. This was her dream now, too, and she was putting everything on the line for it. Once *Grendel* sold, I had the money to buy her a ring and invited her for an evening cruise on a small powerboat along the San Francisco waterfront. It was fairly warm for mid-March, and very clear and calm. I pulled up beside a small fisherman's chapel at Fisherman's Wharf and asked her to marry me. She said yes, and we celebrated with dinner on the wharf.

We decided to have the wedding soon, on July 21, because there were only a few small windows of time available in the first year of our charter schedule.

The next two weeks were busy with planning the wedding and making last-minute arrangements for crew and repairs and insurance, but it all went smoothly. By April 3, when I boarded the plane with Michael Pardee for Spain, everything except the hauling of the boat had worked out perfectly.

Part
Three

THE BOAT DID not look good. The paint job was even worse than I remembered, and rust stains were everywhere. The stern ladder was not out, so we had to board the stern of the next boat and climb over at midships. Standing on my own deck, I was filled with despair. The deck was stained with rust and all of the wood on the huge pilothouse was gray and warped. The wooden rails were completely dried and cracked.

Michael stood on the deck of the other boat, handing our luggage over, and he shook his head. "I don't know, David," he said. "Maybe we should just fly back home."

The feeling of regret was overwhelming. Everything I had done to go back into business. Four months of arrangements. I had already paid almost $30,000 to the marina and the lawyers, and I had signed the new promissory notes.

But the deal was not quite final. The sale and registration had to go through one last office in Gibraltar, so if I was willing to take the $30,000 loss, I could get out of it. I would need to think about this.

In the pilothouse, the loveliest part of the boat, we could see that some of the varnish had been preserved. But not all of it, even on the inside. For a year and four months, salt spray had blown over the breakwater behind us into the pilothouse and down below into the main salon. The throttles and engine panels were rusted and pitted, and both tables, including the large one for sixteen, were weathered gray. Even up high, on the inside of the ceiling, salt crystals had chewed into the varnish. All of this wood would need to be sanded bare and revarnished. Some of it would need to be planed and screwed down where it was warping.

Down below, in the main salon, a damp salt grime coated everything. In every stateroom, too. Lots of mildew. But at least the varnish was okay in the staterooms. And they were beautiful, big staterooms, all solid mahogany.

The engine room was the most depressing. The marina had not kept the water pumped, and it was about three feet deep, just reaching the bottoms of the engines. The water had not reached the starters and alternators, luckily, but my two electric discharge pumps—big expensive pumps—were completely submerged, as was the pump for the saltwater toilet system. And it wasn't just salt water in here. Used oil containers must have floated and tipped over, leaving thick black sludge three feet deep throughout the entire engine room, which was twenty feet wide and fifteen feet long, with steel stringers that had many surfaces, every inch of which would need to be cleaned.

Michael and I began a truly awful month, a month in which I hated every minute of every day and we worked without taking any time off. He was doing this without any compensation, just as a favor to me. And he stuck with me through all of it and even remained cheerful.

In his early sixties and well-off after a lifetime of hard work, Michael had to endure what became a series of privations. We couldn't use the toilets, since the saltwater pump for flushing needed to be replaced. We did have running water, but only a limited supply. We had no heating, and it was cold at night. We had no blankets. We had very little electrical power, since I was still cleaning and drying out the entire system before switching it on.

While we worked, Nick Bushnell was helping set up an appointment at El Rodeo, a marina in Algeciras, across the bay from Gibraltar. The boat needed to be hauled out for rudder modification, bottom cleaning, and new bottom paint. Like Michael, Nick wasn't charging me for his help. He said he just wanted to see it work out for me this time. True generosity. He also found a guy named Stan who would work on the engine room and bilges, and two women to do laundry and clean the staterooms.

Cleaning the engine room was the worst job. Because oil scum floats, most of the water underneath could be pumped out. But that still left about a foot of sludge and all the scum on the walls going up to the three-foot mark. Stan and I went down into it with buckets and mops, filling container after container.

We were covered in black slime. Our tennis shoes were slipping in it, and we had it on our faces and in our hair. The batteries were low, so the lighting was dim, and the water was cold. We mopped and sponged all the angles and surfaces of far too many steel stringers and ribs for about ten hours straight, and when we were through, nothing was clean yet, but the thick sludge was gone.

The next day we used Jif, a household cleaning product that cuts through grease and oil like nothing I've ever witnessed. But it also has ammonia in it, and our engine room blowers weren't working, so the fumes were intense. We suffered from dizziness and headaches throughout the day.

Both sailboats I've owned have probably shortened my lifespan. I may have some significant problems later in life from all the particles and fumes I've inhaled. But each time,

I've felt I had to just keep going, because of money and dead-lines. I had to get this boat ready to sail across the Atlantic in less than a month. The broker in Florida had just booked another charter for us, at the end of July. Nancy and I would be running this charter less than a week after our wedding.

The day after Stan and I finished cleaning the engine room, he began cleaning the aft bilge area and I dismantled the two big discharge pumps that had been submerged. I brought them up on deck, onto the large table, and Michael, when he was done installing his HAM radio, took them apart, piece by piece, and tried to clean them out. Every day I brought him a new item. The two discharge pumps, the two engine room blowers, the saltwater toilet pump, the two extra alternators. All needed drying and cleaning, which meant taking apart and putting back together. Most of them would also need repair in a shop in Gibraltar.

After a week a slip opened up and I was able to move the boat from Sotogrande to Gibraltar. We made slow time toward the eastern side of the Rock, our bottom and props covered with a year and a half of growth, the props most likely encrusted with barnacles. The steering was difficult. But in Gibraltar the facili-ties were better and now we could get our work done. Fred the Perkins dealer inspected the engines first thing the next morning, finding what looked like toothpaste in the port trans-mission. A lot of salt water had gotten into the oil somehow, and it had congealed over time. I felt like a bonehead for not having noticed this myself, but I had checked the transmission oil when the problem first occurred, and the mechanics who had tested the engine over the next week had all missed it.

The good news was that it was a cheap and easy repair. I had budgeted $3,000 for engine repair, but changing the transmission oil a few times was only going to cost about $25. It might also solve my rudder problem. If the transmission was engaging and disengaging randomly because of salt water in its oil, that could throw off the steering.

I also found a shop that looked at my discharge pumps and engine room blowers and other electric-motor problems. All of the equipment was fried because of the salt.

In the rush to get the boat ready on time, many things did not go smoothly. Stan, for instance, the laborer I had hired, overheard me one day when I complained about him to Michael.

"Nothing ever gets done unless I'm here to make sure it gets done," I told Michael. "It's always been like that, in every country. I go out for a few hours to take care of pumps and see the lawyers and buy some engine spares, and when I come back, Stan has been wasting his time, doing stupid shit I didn't ask him to do. When he's finished with one project, he doesn't think. He doesn't remember what I asked him to do next. In Mexico and Turkey, too, no one ever thinks."

Right about then, I heard Stan clear his throat from down in stateroom number three. He had overheard everything I had just said. I was so tired and frustrated and ashamed, I couldn't even do the right thing and apologize. Instead, I took off and ran some more errands.

When I returned, Stan was gone and Michael said I should try to find him in one of the waterfront bars. I went looking but couldn't find him, so I just went back to work. Then, after I had installed the manual bilge pump and was on my way to see Fred, I ran into Michael and Stan sitting at a café. I sat down with them and apologized.

Stan was gracious about it. He was in his late fifties, a guy with bad teeth and a weathered face who had known a series of failures all his life and needed a job but didn't need to be insulted. He leaned back in his chair, smoking, and told me, "It's all right. I appreciate the apology, but it's all right. I can be thick-headed sometimes, and I didn't remember what you had asked for."

"No," I said. "It really is my fault. You work hard, and you do good work."

"Well thank you," he said. "I know how it is. Usually you'd

hire a couple of Moroccans to do this sort of work, I know that. Working for this pay. But I pride myself on trying to do a good job anyway, and I like to feel at the end of the day that I'm someone, too."

I felt awful. His disgusting racist comments aside, he still didn't need to be treated like this by me. I treated him and Michael to a good dinner and some beers, but I felt like human garbage. Stan was living on an old twenty-foot boat in the worst marina in town. At the moment his boat was chained to the dock, impounded for overdue marina fees. And here I was insulting him. The whole situation was lousy, and I didn't know how to fix it. Stan continued working for me, and I was careful never to insult him again, but the damage had been done.

I also began to feel ashamed of the boat. New megayachts were pulling up every day, many of them heading for a big Italian boat show, and we were tied to the back of their dock, an embarrassment with orange streaks down our hull, galvanized rigging that was completely rusted, and warped gray wood on the pilothouse. I was insulting everyone, rich and poor alike.

The work was getting done, however. I was leaving all cosmetic work for Trinidad, despite the embarrassment, but I was completing the functional work now, before the crossing.

Our last week was busy. We had four volunteer crew arriving, and they all worked hard. We installed the new rigging wires, inspected the sails, stenciled the new name on the stern, cleaned and organized the galley, took care of plumbing problems, mounted new pumps, and even bought a washer/dryer and stowed it in the engine room.

Five more crew members arrived at the end, including my uncle Doug. I was excited to have Doug on board. We had been out of touch for more than ten years after my father's death, but had since reconciled. Now I really enjoyed seeing him, and this was our chance to spend some time together. I was also hoping to hear more about my father's commercial fishing venture, since Doug had been his crew.

The night before we left I didn't sleep well. I was thinking about my decision to go back into business, to try the boat a second time. The bankruptcy had separated me from any liability; I could have walked away. I had chosen to try a second time because I didn't want to leave my lenders in the lurch and because I thought everything could work out. I was smarter about running the business, and I had much easier financing. But now that I was here, working on the boat, about to sail across the Atlantic, I didn't feel the dream. The boat and the business were recoverable, but not the dream.

WE SET SAIL on May 2, on a sunny morning with light winds. We unfurled our jib right away, setting the tone for a trip we hoped would be more sailing than motoring. The channel was much calmer than during my previous attempts, and we made it past the final lighthouse on the Moroccan coast without incident.

That night, however, in about the same position where I had lost my rudder a year and a half earlier, the wind and waves came up and slapped us around. Then we heard a loud metallic booming sound in our stern area.

"Not again," I said. Everyone woke up and came on deck, and we began checking. We weren't spinning, so we still had a rudder.

"It could be the port transmission," I said. "If it has salt water in it again and slipped. Or maybe something hit the prop. I don't really know."

My crew stayed calm, and we checked everything. It was the middle of the night, no moon, and the wind and seas were building. I checked the oil in the port transmission, felt for heat on the shaft glands, listened from the aft stateroom for sounds of a bent shaft as we turned at various revolutions, checked the hydraulic ram under the bed, tried the handling and speed and gauges at the helm. But everything checked out fine.

"We must have just hit a big piece of wood or something," I told the crew.

I went back to bed, but it was too weird. To have the same type of sound at the same time of night in the same place in the ocean, a year and a half later. I sometimes felt like Oedipus, running and running and escaping nothing.

We continued on to Las Palmas in the Canary Islands without any problems. The three and a half days underway were entirely pleasant. And we had a good time in Las Palmas. There are several long stretches of beach with hotels and restaurants built along a boardwalk, and one night we all became pleasantly lost in the twists and turns between bays and beaches. We had a feast at one of the restaurants, confusing each other's orders, gorging from tapas and pizzas and entrées. We had too much wine and were talking too loud and poking fun at each other. Then we got lost again and straggled back to the boat.

There were also some interesting people to meet on the dock. My uncle Doug and I were busy the first day just cleaning up the engine room, because during the trip a fitting on the copper return line for one of the diesels had leaked and diesel had sprayed everywhere. Our many trips to the waste disposal took us past an old wooden schooner that was being restored, and we met an interesting captain. He had restored almost a dozen of these old boats. By the time we left, he had lent us a drill bit (which we broke and replaced with bottles of wine), we had swapped navigation books, and I had tried unsuccessfully to steal his best carpenter. All in good fun.

Leaving Las Palmas, we were sailing. The wind was good. But that night it increased significantly. We left up our full main and genoa, but the wind was gusting over thirty knots.

I enjoyed the speed, but I could see that several of the crew just couldn't handle the steering. I needed to drop our main.

We furled our genoa first, then headed into the wind. We let the halyard go, but the sail stuck high in the track. Seref had attached the track in two pieces, and the place where the two tracks joined sometimes jammed the cars. So here I was at night in seas and wind, the sail whipping wildly, making sounds like pistol shots, and it wouldn't come down.

I tried pulling the sail from the aft end, which meant climbing onto the roof of the pilothouse, a dangerous spot in the high wind and seas. Two of my crew were at the halyard, pulling it up, then releasing it, over and over, but that wasn't doing any good either. Finally I went forward to the mainmast and climbed fifteen feet off the deck, to where I could grab on to a fold of the sail. I held on with both hands, let my feet dangle above the deck, and started yanking downward with all my body weight and strength while my crew kept tightening and releasing the halyard.

Even as I was doing this, I realized it might not be very safe. The deck was rolling, it was dark, we were being blasted with salt water and howling wind, and I was dangling above the deck, yanking on something that would eventually give way. There were winches and other metal fittings I might hit on the way down, a lot of things to land on that weren't soft. But I just did it, frustrated with the stupidity of having a mainsail that wouldn't come down.

And then the sail fell, all in an instant, and I fell fast and hard, clipping my knee on a stainless fitting on the mast. I rolled on the deck, threw out my arms to find something to hold on to, and found a bulwark for the forward seating area. I paused, wondering how hard I had hit, and then stood up. The knee was sore, but I could stand and walk, so I was okay.

A day and a half later, in predawn darkness, we slowed and waited in a large channel outside our port in the Cape Verde

Islands. This was Africa. I had passed within sight of several African ports on my way across the Mediterranean a year and a half earlier, but this was going to be my first time actually landing in an African country. The guidebooks all warned to stop for fuel and nothing more. The crime rate, especially theft from visiting yachts, was supposed to be horrific.

The wind made it cold out in the channel. The waves were up, too, as they always are in channels, and the crew was ready for a break from the rolling, even if only for a few hours. We continued to wait, though, because I didn't want to enter this unfamiliar port at night. The charts for it were not good, and I had no other knowledge to draw on.

The sky went from black to a very dark blue, then gradually lightened. We began to see the outline of mountains, the eastern sky behind them a paler blue. And then we could see land masses around the lights of the port, a large rock in the center of the bay and, as we approached slowly, the long line of a breakwater down low.

I tried the VHF, but no one responded. It was early on a Saturday. We crept closer and found ourselves in a little bay that was shallowing, with no fuel dock in sight and a few rocks just sticking up randomly, unmarked, so I turned us around, back toward the commercial docks, and decided to tie up next to the ships.

A man came jogging down the dock, waving for us to pull alongside. He wasn't wearing a uniform, so he was just a local guy looking for a tip, but I was willing to take whatever help I could find.

We docked in a strong surge, greeted with a lot of words that were in English but difficult to understand, and I went ashore with my new guide and our passports and boat papers.

This town looked like a Mexican port town, the nearby hills sharp and dry, a desert with banded rock. Along the waterfront was the main road and boardwalk, with some palm trees. The town itself very sleepy. A few historical buildings and shops that were painted but most of the rest needing some work. A lot of concrete. What was different, of course, was the entirely black population, and all the details of their daily lives, from the stands at each corner selling thimblefuls of a local alcohol that looked thick and sweet to the vendors from other African countries spreading their wares on the side-walks. Carved animals and rough iron products. I followed my guide but was distracted all along the way, wanting to soak up as much of this new place as I possibly could in a few hours.

My guide did not have a high reputation in the town. At the first stand we passed, he tried to bum one cigarette, since cigarettes were sold individually rather than by the pack, and he pointed to me as credit but still was refused. I didn't inter-vene. I was going to pay him $20 at the end of the day, which was more than the local wages for a week's work, and that was good enough. I didn't want to become entangled in any local dealings.

It was hard not to, though. My guide was telling me his life story and introducing me to people, and the government offices weren't open yet, so we had some time to kill. We went into a large market building, where several dozen women stood at their stalls selling grains and vegetables, local honey and nuts and fruit and the local alcohol. Several tried to get me to try this stuff, and I kept resisting, but finally one woman basically poured a shot-glass of it into my mouth, which annoyed me con-siderably. The drink was both sugary and very high proof.

The fruit and vegetables were beautiful and strange, things I had never seen. The women were beautiful, too. One in par-ticular I must have stared at twice, when I first walked in and when I walked out. She looked at me in a very hostile way that seemed to double as an invitation. It was something I didn't know how to read.

I did get back on track for finding the diesel. My guide had acquired several things by now, a small bottle of the alcohol and some nuts and a few cigarettes, trading on what I would pay him in the afternoon, and he was not letting up on the stories, either, most of which I didn't understand. I did understand that he was not living with either of the two women he had married, and that he had several children and wanted to do great things for them. He had also gone to sea, working on a small local freighter that was in constant danger of capsizing. He spoke of crooked politicians and a murder that had taken place on the docks, and he spoke of the lush, green tropical mountains that were just beyond the ones we could see from the town. I would have to come back, he said, and he would take me into these mountains. They were beautiful, not dry and barren like the ones I could see.

I came to like my guide, not for anything he had done, since he was obviously of low repute and a bit shifty, with a life that had been in ruin for years, but because he was a reminder that we are constantly inventing and reinventing ourselves, and he put no limits on how good or generous he could be in other circumstances. I believed him in this. I, too, had dreams of being generous, of giving to my family and friends if I ever made it, of helping people who needed help. But I was always behind budget and struggling financially, the business always not making it, so at this point I'm sure most people regarded me warily. I wanted to prove them wrong. I wanted to be a good and generous man, and I think this man, my guide, wanted the same things. Probably neither of us would ever realize the dream, but that didn't make the dreaming any less pure.

The open mid-Atlantic was not quite what any of us had expected. Overcast and muggy, with very little breeze. We kept our sails out almost the entire eleven days, but we also had one engine on.

Every night, the sky cleared and the stars were brilliant. But then every morning, the haze moved in again and the skies became overcast. The seas were also monotonous, never calm but never rough, holding at no more than ten feet.

The enjoyable part of the trip for me was spending time with my uncle. At first this was while playing cards and during mealtimes and watches at the helm. But then, halfway through the trip, we began sanding the outside of the pilot-house, getting a jump on all the work to be done in Trinidad. I led with a belt sander, tearing down through old varnish, gray wood, and warped seams with rough, fifty-grit belts. My uncle followed using an orbital sander with eighty-grit disks, the first step toward smoothing the surface.

We baked in the sun, covered in reddish dust, and discussed the possibilities for the business. Schools of flying fish skimmed the water. The haze sometimes cleared away later in the afternoon, leaving a sky deep blue and enormous. It was the way we had first known each other, when I was a child and we had hunted or fished with my father, out in a wild land so beautiful, whether it was Alaska or California. We had fished for king salmon or stood at the tops of ridges scanning for bucks or wild boar. This would become one of those times.

But now we understood each other better. This business was my chance to escape wage labor and never getting ahead. I could net $300,000 a year, working only twenty weeks, as my own boss. Doug had seen my father try making a living on the water, too, had worked alongside him, and though it hadn't panned out in the end, Doug considered the venture a success because of the experiences they had shared. It had been wonderful and strange.

One night in the Bering Sea, their compass and electronics had shown them spinning in a slow circle, though the rudder was dead center and they were making way on what should have been a straight course. There was no explanation for it. They tried the helm and the rudder was working, but they were slowly being pulled into a vortex. The only possible explanations, it seemed, were supernatural. It was night, of course, and they were a hundred miles from land and the seas were building. That is always the case when something goes wrong with a boat.

Finally my uncle went out on deck, just to see, though he had no idea what he was looking for. He staggered back and forth in the rain and seas and then saw one of the stabilizers pulled out at a sharp angle, the entire boat heeling that way. They were snagged on something, out in the deep ocean.

Imagination suggested sea monsters and lost cities, but when my father stopped the engines and the boat slowed, they found the stabilizer caught on a large buoy that had dragged them in circles. It was a navigational buoy that had come loose and was drifting. Now it all made sense, but those minutes of not knowing had been unforgettable. Mystery in the world. The two of them out there alone, wondering if their lives would soon be ended.

What I enjoyed most was the new portrait of my father that was emerging. For at least fifteen years after his suicide, I had been very angry at him, hating him for abandoning me and for killing himself in such a dirty, shameful way, blowing his own head off. But now, after my bankruptcy and all of my other smaller frustrations and failures in this business, I could see a man struggling, a man who had been almost exactly my age, who had shared a similar dream of wanting to be able to invent his own life, instead of going every day to a job he hated, a man drawn to the same frontier.

My uncle had also been angry at my father, and for the first ten or fifteen years after my father's suicide, he fought constant depression. But now he could appreciate the times he'd shared with my father and see him in a more generous light.

My uncle was also able to see me more generously. When I was growing up, he resented that my mother and sister and I had a bit more money than he did, and since my mother didn't make me work during high school, he felt I never learned to work hard. But now he could see I did know how to work hard. And he could see that we enjoyed the same sense of adventure.

One morning we worked for hours on an unusual cooling problem in one of the engines and finally found the inexplicable, a piece of seaweed so large it could not have traveled through all the various strainers to where we found it. Yet there it was. Laughing with him at the absurdity of this, I could have been crew on my father's boat twenty-five years earlier.

This voyage was easy. A scoop of ice cream each night in the big pilothouse, card games and dice, reading, great conversation, music. But easy as it was, by the time we neared Trinidad, everyone was ready for land. I spotted Tobago in the distance at daybreak. Lush mountains, colorful homes, a tropical paradise. We continued on until Trinidad came into view, and then we cruised along its northern coast. Very rugged and mountainous, like the northern coast of Kauai. There were thousands of small jellyfish in the water, and one of our crew, Mary Helen, who was a marine biologist, told us about drift science.

The most famous "experiment" in drift science involved tennis shoes. A cargo ship had accidentally dumped thousands of new tennis shoes overboard, and for many months afterward, as these tennis shoes traveled the world, managing for the most part to stay together, scientists followed them. The tennis shoes were not strong swimmers, and they were not known to communicate with each other or to have any organizational structure, so they were a good model for studying jellyfish migration. They stayed together unbelievably well, despite storms and currents and everything else.

Several of us accused Mary Helen of making this up, but she insisted it was true. She did admit, however, that jellyfish were, in the final analysis, more complicated in their migrations than tennis shoes. They didn't drift only with the surface current. Around bays, for instance, they could descend to a level where current would bring them back in after they had drifted out. They could seek salinity or temperature or current bands. They were able, in response to a will even more opaque than our own, to control their drift.

ALWAYS A STRANGE experience, riding a boat twenty-five feet above land, seeming to fly, and stranger still for our destination. Sand everywhere, a small Sahara, the blasters and painters in full suits with hoods, a toxic waste crew wandering this industrial desert endlessly. Downwind of us, toward the water, was nothing nice. Some huge round cement containers, an abandoned field, then industrial docks. I hadn't thought much about blasting before, even when I had decided to do it, but I realized now it would send up a constant cloud of epoxy filler, paint, and steel mixed in with the sand. My uncle and I had prepared all of this wood for varnishing, but I could see now we weren't going to be doing any varnishing until we left the blasting yard.

Before we could blast, we had to remove the wooden railing from the boat. This was not easy; the rails were glued down as well as bolted. Ducky, the foreman of the blasting company, decided we needed hydraulic jacks, and he drove me toward Port of Spain, the capital, in his beat-up little car. We passed roadside markets, like corner stores, made of brightly painted plywood and concrete. Trinidad looked much more third-world than I had expected. I asked Ducky how much the houses cost and he whistled and said they had gone way up. Almost 300,000 TT now for one of the nicer homes. That was a bit less than $50,000 U.S. I tried to explain that a small three-bedroom house where I was from, on the peninsula south of San Francisco, now cost about $800,000 U.S., but it sounded so crazy that he didn't believe me. He asked how much money I could make in the United States, and when I told him I had made $27,000 a year teaching full-time at Stanford, he didn't believe that, either.

"That mean you have no *way* of buying a house," he said.

I told him that was true. That was part of the point of my trying this whole boating business. If I didn't try something other than being a lecturer, I'd be renting overpriced apartments until I died, and I would never save a penny. I told him an unremarkable one-person apartment cost more than $1,500 a month, but I could tell he didn't quite believe this, either. The world I came from was, in fact, insane. Here in Trinidad, Ducky could make the equivalent of $15,000 U.S. a year, working very hard, and buy a good house for the equivalent of $50,000. His life made sense.

We stopped at a shop for auto parts, where I bought three small hydraulic jacks, then returned to the boat.

Seref had glued these rails never to come off, which didn't make sense, since he hadn't bothered to properly coat the steel beneath. When we finally made it to the aft rails on our second day of work, there was only primer beneath, if even that. Seref had done nothing to protect the steel. Just slapped the wood on and lied to me.

Ducky and one of his crew suited up at dawn the next morning, wearing hoods that had air blowing in through a small hose. This created a positive pressure seal from inside and was the only way to keep out sand, epoxy, and paint. They wore heavy gloves and boots, but the high-pressure air and sand coming out of the blasting hose was capable of cutting through a boot almost instantly.

Sandblasting is truly industrial. The sound of these hoses was like the roar of jet engines, and the dust billowed out in clouds for hundreds of feet. I was up on deck when they began blasting, and I had every incentive to get my work done quickly. Even with a respirator and earplugs and goggles, the sand and epoxy dust and sound were getting in.

When I finally climbed the twenty-five feet down to the ground, two hours later, I could see their progress. Gray tracks across the red-painted underbody. Ducky held the hose in both hands and clamped it with his legs. He used short up-and-down movements to work away at the paint. The toughest areas were the ones with deep epoxy filler; the filler makes the sand bounce.

Bare steel is gray and porous, super dry and capable of quickly soaking up any moisture. The biggest challenge for a good blasting job is the weather. If it rains, the steel immediately rusts and has to be reblasted. Even too much humidity can start the rust. And this was almost the beginning of the rainy season. We were right on the edge. It could start raining any day and not let up for weeks.

I was negotiating with KNJ, the yard's painting company, over the paint job, and this went on and on. I tried hard to keep the negotiations friendly. I wanted to enjoy the business this time. During my year of working for the dot-com, I missed Turkey and all the other places I'd been, and I wished I'd relaxed and enjoyed all of it more. I had been tense the entire summer in Turkey while the boat was being finished and launched. There had been a lot of problems, and I had let them get to me instead of enjoying that magnificent place and the adventure of what I was doing. I wanted this time to be different.

KNJ slowly came around. Nigel, the painter, looked at the job again, knowing I wasn't going to pay the price he'd quoted, and agreed to a lower amount. So once the blasting, priming, epoxy, and bottom paint were finished, the travelift picked up the boat again, and I sailed over the dusty sea to Nigel's trailer in a corner of Peake's yard. Scaffolding went up immediately, which Nigel tried to get me to pay for, since it was rented from the yard. I said no, annoyed that he was already trying to nickel-and-dime me, and he just smiled. I hoped this kind of thing wouldn't continue.

Nigel had a partner, Davey, and a crew of about ten other guys. They began with microballoons, which are microscopic glass bubbles mixed in an epoxy paste. The microballoons form a super hard shell over the steel, almost like another hull, which can be sanded down for a more even surface. This was what the faring was all about. Trying to turn my patchwork of welding seams into something smooth, "like an egg," as Seref had said.

I wouldn't get to know this crew the way I had gotten to know Ducky's crew. I had a long list of things to fix or buy while in Trinidad. And the wood my uncle and I had sanded had turned from light red to dark gray in just one week. The sun was so hot that raw wood darkened in a single day.

I was in the Internet cafés every evening, keeping in touch with our clearinghouse in the Virgin Islands and the broker in Florida. The broker sold another trip for us in November, and another in February, bringing the total to five charters. If I could just get the boat fixed up and delivered on time, we were going to do well. We'd pay off most of our credit cards by January, and we'd have another full year before starting monthly payments to our lienholders. This was a pleasant change, having a business with a bright future.

But at the moment cash was tight and I was trying to get deals on everything while Nancy, back in California, was working and applying for more credit cards. I did a lot of negotiating, playing at least three local vendors off each other for every large item, working the price lower and lower, hoofing back and forth, pissing off a few people but staying on budget.

Each night I dragged a mattress up to sleep on deck amid the epoxy and paint dust, hoping the toxins weren't taking years off my life. It was hot as hell, and muggy. There were mosquitos, so I had to put a sheet over me, including my head, and sleep in an oven. It was bright from the yard lights and noisy from traffic passing on the road. One of my neighbors liked to play soca music most nights between 2 A.M. and 4 A.M., and a group of prostitutes liked to yell up at me from the other side of the yard's fence. So I didn't sleep very well. I used the yard showers and bathrooms, ordered sandwiches from the local restaurant, and peed off the deck into the yard.

Nancy joined me for the last two weeks of June and the first week of July, a welcome relief even though we were both working full-time on the varnish. We were about to be married, and it was a wonderful time to be together, even in an industrial wasteland.

We hired two of the painters after hours and weekends to help us, and one of them, Stephen, we came to like and trust enormously. We hired him as crew to sail to the Virgin Islands and run our first two charters, and he started to tell us the truth about what Nigel and Davey were doing on the paint job. Davey was his friend, and a good guy, but Nigel was starting to cut corners.

Nigel was running out of money for materials. He had the paint already, but he was running short on filler for the final stages of faring. He claimed this was because he had under-quoted the job, and the painting company backed him up on this, but one afternoon I saw him installing a new stereo system in his car, and it looked to me as if he had just spent too much of the money. I had paid the full bill up front. Stephen kept telling me this had been a mistake, that you never pay more than half up front in Trinidad if you want the job done, but I hadn't had a choice. I had some very touchy finances.

My relationship with Nigel deteriorated quickly. He reminded me more and more of Seref. He was cavalier about problems that he said would be fixed later, such as the white dots all over my teak deck and windlass from overspray. I was seeing a lot of big jobs being saved for later, and later was drawing near.

Nancy and I had originally planned a few weekends to tour Trinidad, but as it turned out, we took only one day off, a Sunday to watch Stephen play cricket. He kept pressing me to take a day off, since I hadn't had one in over three months. "You too stressed," he told me. "Pressure, boy, pressure."

Stephen picked us up in the morning. He had promised I would be able to play today, which I was excited about, though I could see I wasn't properly dressed. Everyone wore white jerseys and white slacks.

Just before the game began, I was invited into a concrete room underneath the stands with Stephen's team. The men stood in a circle, and the team captain welcomed me as a friend of Stephen's. He talked about the importance of today's match, which was against a fierce rival, and went through a prayer and proceeded to give a lot of mixed messages about it being just a game, for fun, but also being gravely important and revealing something about who they were as people and as a community and whether they'd be able to continue to hold their heads high after this day when they walked around their neighborhood. I was starting to realize that cricket is a serious sport in Trinidad, and I wasn't surprised to hear at the end of the speech that I would be well represented on the field by Stephen, which was a lovely, diplomatic way of saying there was no way the captain was going to let some newcomer screw up this important match.

So Nancy and I sat and watched for hours. Cricket is not an exciting spectator sport. Friends of Stephen's did explain the rules, so we could know what was going on, and Stephen played well, and in what was apparently an exciting match by cricket standards, his team prevailed.

When the game ended, after something like five hours, the speeches resumed and continued until long after dark. I have never encountered another culture so fond of speech-making. Each team had at least five or six dignitaries who made speeches. The second speech, by Stephen's team captain, accepting the victory and the trophy, praised the good fortune given by God and praised individual players for various feats of heroism and went into a long, spiraling history of the team and the opposing team and how they were really the same team, sharing some players over the years, and how basically everyone here in Trinidad and maybe on God's green earth was all part of the same team, though this particular team, on this particular day, had shown its mettle and gained a great victory, which would be remembered, etc., and then, as he was wrapping up, he mentioned that we were all very honored today to have celebrities among us, who had honored us all by coming to watch today's game. He pointed up into the stands behind us, and we were very excited, turning around to find these celebrities. But there was no one behind us. We were the celebrities. We finally stood, since that was what they expected, and waved.

KNOWING NOW THAT we were celebrities, it was hard to go back to the same old crap in Peake's yard. Nigel was careless about overspray, he was running short on materials, and he still hadn't started the bowsprit. Nancy flew home to take care of final arrangements for our July 21 wedding in California, and I tried to get the boat finished. I needed to sail to the Virgin Islands very soon.

This last week pushed me close to the edge. My friend Galen flew in from Hawaii to help. He had offered me a choice of this or coming to my wedding. But there was still too much to do. Oil changes late at night, working on pumps and valves and lights, getting ready to go back into the water. I was also scrambling to finish the varnish, with help from Stephen. I was almost completely out of cash. But what was taking up too much of my time was the paint job.

In addition to overspray and materials problems, Nigel was trying to cheat me on the topcoats. To save time and material, he sprayed two thin coats on the starboard side on the same day, rather than on two consecutive days with a light scuff between. This left dry patches and drip marks. Stephen pointed them out to me, after hours, and said I should insist Nigel respray that side. And on the other side of the boat, Nigel hadn't brought the faring down low enough. I had pointed it out to him many times, but he didn't catch on until too late. Then he tried to argue that the two stripes at the waterline weren't included in the price, and he drew one of them with a large sag.

To mark the waterline of a hull and its boot-stripes, long pieces of tape are pulled. A man stands on scaffolding and brings his hand across sideways, keeping it level, so that the tape naturally conforms to the curve of the hull at the same height. Nigel claimed to be a master at drawing a waterline, and he had a guy named Michael working for him who was also supposed to be a master, but when I looked at the bow from a hundred yards away, I could see clearly that the line on the starboard side had a long dip to it, about twenty feet long.

I pointed this out to Nigel, and he ignored me, so I pointed it out to Michael, then Davey, then went to KNJ. It was very frustrating. I remember standing out in the yard with Nigel, showing it to him. The sag so obviously there, and Nigel beside me telling me I'm seeing things, that it's just a trick of light on the curve of the hull. He held up his two hands, one of them the smooth side of my boat, the other feeling this surface. "The hull come out, but your eye get tricked. Your eye think the hull go in."

Under pressure from KNJ he was forced to redraw the line, but he drew it again with the same sag. I was forced to accept it because I had no more time.

Then the blasting company came to finish painting the bulwarks and forward seating area, but the crew was young and didn't tape properly. They left drops of paint all over the teak deck.

My friend Galen was much calmer about all of this than I

was, until one day he felt I was ordering him around too much. He finally blew up, basically telling me that our friendship was more important than this paint job and I needed to work on how I was addressing him.

"No," I told him. "You're wrong. You don't get to feel upset. You don't get the luxury of yelling at me or making me think about your feelings. You haven't been working all day every fucking day for months to get this boat ready. You haven't invested $100,000 this year. You didn't sail across the ocean. You're not responsible for anything. It's not your neck if this boat doesn't arrive in the Virgin Islands on time. And I don't have time to deal with your feelings. I have too much other shit to deal with. If you don't like it, fly home."

I was losing it. Galen and I had grown up together. He was the first person to whom I had been able to tell the truth about my father (I told everyone at school he had died of cancer). But now I had to get the boat done, and I just didn't have even five minutes to discuss Galen's feelings.

Later that day, Galen actually apologized to me, which was amazing. Most people would have called me an asshole and left.

It's difficult to express the chaos of the last days in the yard. It just went on and on.

We went back in the water on a Friday afternoon so we could spend the weekend in the "well," as they call the water underneath the travelift. We were still bolting the rails, stanchions, and other fittings, and we still had a lot of work to do on the varnish.

The teak rails were actually iroko, similar to teak, and it turns out I'm extremely allergic to iroko dust. My eyes and lips puffed up from the sanding and I had red rashes all over my chest and neck, which was a nice addition to how I felt about everything.

The next morning, I went to customs and immigration to clear us out. We were going to sail the following day, Sunday, July 15. That would get us to the Virgin Islands by the eighteenth, a day before my flight home to get married. But when the large man at the immigration counter looked over my paperwork, he said I needed my former crew to appear in person to be removed from the boat's entrance papers.

"They're gone," I said. "I apologize, but I didn't know they had to come here before they left the country. They cleared immigration and customs at the airport."

"Every crew member need to clear out before the vessel can leave."

"They did clear out, but at the airport."

"They need to clear out here first, to be removed from your paperwork."

"I didn't know this," I said.

"You know this. We tellin' everyone when they clears in."

"But I wasn't told. I really wasn't. I'm very careful about these things."

"You cannot clear out until all of these crew members present themselves."

"But they're all in the U.S. now."

The man paused. He was a very large black man with glasses. He looked hassled. I was trying to be polite, but I needed him to let me leave. "You can pay the fine that's two thousand five hundred dollars U.S. per person," he said. "Or you can provide proof that they left the country, by givin' me their flight numbers and dates, then I need to confirm those clearances with the central office."

"But I need to leave tomorrow," I told him. "I'm getting married. I'll miss my own wedding if I can't leave."

"I tellin' you the two options, sir. Your crew need to clear out before they leave."

"But no one told me. Are you really going to make me do this?"

"I tellin' you already."

"I can't pay the fines," I said. "I honestly don't have the money. I really don't. I spent everything here getting work done. And now I need to leave."

He just looked at me, unwilling to budge.

"Okay," I said. "If I make calls right now and get you the flight numbers, how long will it take to verify with the central office?"

"They not open 'til Monday, and then it take three or four hours."

"Monday!" I said. "I can't leave Monday. I'll miss my own wedding. And I came in here yesterday to clear, on a weekday, a Friday, just in case there were any problems, and I was told to come back today, Saturday, because a clearance can't be done more than twenty-four hours in advance."

"That's correct."

"But don't you see, I've been caught in a trap. No one told me about the regulation when I cleared in. Then, when I tried to clear out early, on a weekday, I wasn't allowed to clear. Now, it's a weekend, and the office isn't open. So I need you to help me find a solution. I need to leave tomorrow."

This man just looked down at his nails, which were long and painted purple. They were so long they curled. Strange with an immigration uniform. He wanted me to go away, but he wasn't willing to sign my form.

Another customer came in then, a European man in his fifties. The guy behind the counter switched his attention to this new man, and took his papers. I waited politely, and after about fifteen minutes, when they were done, I tried again.

"Please," I said. "I'm very sorry that my former crew didn't follow the regulations, but we honestly didn't know. And I'm sorry if I've offended you in any other way. I certainly haven't meant to. Please let me clear out. I really have to leave."

"Eight A.M. Monday morning," he told me.

Galen and Stephen and our other new crew member, Donna, were sitting in folding chairs behind me, listening to all of this. None of them could do anything to help. The Trinis, as Trinidadians call themselves, were of course afraid of their own immigration and customs officials.

We left and went immediately to an Internet café a few doors down. "If I can't get this info on time," I told Galen and Stephen and Donna, "we're just leaving anyway. And you might as well go back to the boat now. I might be a while."

After I'd sent my e-mails and made my calls, I walked back to the boat and seriously considered just leaving. To hell with Trinidad. I would never be able to come back into this country, but maybe that was okay. By the time I reached the boat, however, I had calmed down, and I reassured the crew that I wouldn't leave until I had clearance. Stephen and Donna looked relieved.

I tried to put the immigration fiasco behind me. We would use our extra day to good advantage, to get more work done, especially on the wood in the forward seating area and on the rails, and as long as I left by around noon on Monday, I could make it to the Virgin Islands just in time, arriving the morning of the day I would fly.

Monday morning, however, presented a new problem. During my entire seven weeks in Trinidad, the wind had been calm in the early morning. But not this morning. It was blowing at over thirty knots and coming from an unusual direction, which happened to be exactly the worst direction possible. I needed to back out of the well, which had high concrete docks on each side, then there were pilings on my port side extending another several hundred feet. The wind would be blowing me directly onto them.

I talked with the crane operator about this. He was not happy.

"You leavin' now, ya. I got other boats." He was white, with long curly blond hair, but he had grown up here.

"I'm sorry," I said. "I know there are boats waiting to be hauled out. But I can't safely leave the dock in this wind. If I try to leave, I will most likely take out your pilings and the big motoryacht behind them. Every other early morning the wind has been low. But this morning, it's high for some reason."

"You leavin'," he said. I could tell he was getting pissed off.

"Please," I said. "As a licensed captain, I can't do something that I know will endanger my boat and other boats. I'm really sorry, but I just can't."

This stand-off kept me from going to immigration and customs. We waited for the wind to die down, but it kept blowing hard. Peake's office called me in, charged me an extra fifty bucks for my time in the well, and demanded I leave.

Finally, another captain offered to help by pushing my bow away from the pilings with his dinghy while I backed, so I agreed to try. When the captain in the dingy and the marina guys on the dock were ready, I shouted "Okay!" and put both engines in hard reverse. The heavy steel hull started sliding back right away, the engines strong, and the bow line and stern lines were both loosed, but then a guy on the stern line, on the dock, wrapped the end of the line around a cleat. He may have thought he was helping me swing my stern out, but what he did was disastrous.

The stern line went tight and yanked my stern upwind. My bow swung down fast, about to bash hard against the concrete dock and crush the dinghy underneath, but luckily the guys on the dock with the bow line saw what was going on and rushed to wrap the end of their line just in time to make the bow bounce. Then the stern line snapped in half and my stern was free, so I had to go. I threw the port engine in reverse again and yelled and waved for the bow to be let go. It was, just in time, and Galen and Stephen were hauling in the lines as I gunned the engines in full reverse, smoke in the air. It was my only chance, to just go as hard and fast as possible. I was also swinging the helm, trying to straighten us out. I could hear a guy on the big powerboat behind the pilings to our port side yelling, "Go! Go! Go!" If I didn't get out of there fast, I was going to destroy his yacht.

We cleared the pilings and then I threw the engines into forward, to stop our momentum, and spun the wheel. There was a crowd of boats anchored right behind us, and I missed one by less than ten feet. I got us out of there, through the crowd to the outer harbor, then I put the engines in neutral and just shook my head. Such a brilliant decision, going back into the boating business.

Four hours later, I finally had my paperwork from immigration and customs. We raised anchor and motored toward "the mouth of the dragon," the narrow channel where we'd leave the island and encounter the ocean. It was after 5:30 P.M., the sun low on the horizon, and we had almost nothing stowed. We weren't ready for a passage. Stephen was putting tools away in boxes, trying to clear the pilothouse, and Galen was stowing the fenders. Donna was not really doing anything except standing around awkwardly.

We reached the mouth in about ten minutes, the big rollers coming in, spray hitting the rocks on the western side. We weren't ready for this. So I turned around, back into calmer water, and did circles for about twenty minutes while I helped stow.

I have never left for sea so unprepared. We had our basic items stowed, and I had completed all of the maintenance and systems checks in previous days, and Donna had bought provisions, and we had enough diesel and water. So it was safe to leave, and we were seaworthy, but it was almost dark, none of my crew had ever been on a passage or at sea at night, we still had various little items inside and out that weren't organized or stowed very well, and we were all exhausted. Not a good way to begin almost three days at sea.

And the seas hit us right away, then built through the night, the wind howling. We were blasting into large waves, the spray covering the entire boat each time. Everyone except me was seasick, so I had to pull double watches at the helm and be on call the entire time. It was a long night.

The daytime was easier for the crew, and we were making

almost ten knots, which was what we needed. We had to average at least eight and a half for me to catch my flight to California. If anything went wrong or we didn't steer well or the seas increased, I would miss my flight and wouldn't be able to catch another flight until the next day, so I'd miss the rehearsal dinner. But if I couldn't get on that flight the next day, if there were no seats available through standby, I'd miss the wedding.

As soon as it was dark again, though, Stephen and Donna couldn't steer. Donna would stand there at the helm looking calm and poised. And she'd be sixty degrees off course, taking us to Europe. Stephen was even worse. He tried hard, and I spent a lot of time tutoring him, but he kept getting disoriented. He would see the compass dial start to spin to the left, so he would turn to the right. This was backward. He did it over and over, spinning us in a circle each time.

I tried to make it simple. "Steer to our heading," I said. "Forget about how the dial is moving. Find two hundred fifty degrees. That's our course. Just steer toward it. Just like lining up a car on the road."

But it didn't work. He kept steering exactly the wrong way. Instead of making almost ten knots on course, we were now averaging only seven and a half, which meant I would miss my wedding.

So Galen and I took over. No more Stephen or Donna at the helm. I didn't have an autopilot, and this meant Galen and I would have to steer around the clock for the next day and a half, alternating with ninety-minute watches. I also needed to check all the boat systems, so I wouldn't sleep more than half an hour at a time. I had done it before, on other passages, but I hadn't begun those trips so tired.

Everything went fine, however. The seas and wind died down, we stayed on course and made good time, and it looked like we were just going to make it.

THE DARK MASSES of the small islands around us, cut out against the stars and lights on Tortola, were a pirate's landscape, and the night air was moist and warm, tropical but not stifling like Trinidad. It was cooler here, with a fresher breeze. I had a beautiful ninety-foot yacht, a promising business, and the freedom to cruise these islands with Nancy for as many years as we wished. It was a good feeling.

I crossed through the pass and the channel and slowly entered the bay at Roadtown. There were a lot of lights, and everything was unfamiliar. Avoiding reefs, shallow water, and boats at anchor, I found the small entrance into the marinas, but once we were in, there seemed to be almost no room, especially after being at sea.

A 90-foot boat with a 21.5-foot beam and 9-foot draft in a small harbor at night feels very large, like a great whale come into a pond. The harbor was actually capable of accommodating larger boats, of course, but it felt like I had almost no room to maneuver. I found Village Cay Marina to my port side, made a 90-degree turn, and proceeded cautiously into a slip on the inside of their fuel dock. It was about 4:30 A.M., and I was going to be able to attend my rehearsal dinner and wedding.

We were married by one of my lenders, a Dominican friar. I'm not Catholic, but Nancy is. The chapel was part of a monastery, rarely used for weddings, the high-backed pews facing inward toward the aisle, their dark wood ornately carved.

Dave, the friar and also my friend, was funny during the ceremony. He said he wouldn't presume to tell us about storms at sea but carried on with his metaphor anyway. The entire event was much more emotional than I had imagined. Somehow I had thought I would just breeze through it, but the truth is I had difficulty not sobbing at various points, especially when we left the altar to greet our parents and my mother whispered in my ear, "Your father and I are both very proud of you." Bringing my father into this, especially with my uncle Doug standing there beside my mother, was overwhelming. One of the saddest parts of my father's death has always been the thought of all that he has missed. Twenty-one years of experience and memories. And each time I thought of him during some important event such as this, my wedding day, his absence hurt just as much as the first day I had lost him. I was thirteen again and didn't have a father.

In the limo, Nancy and I both admitted surprise at how emotional the ceremony had been, but then we moved on to the reception and just had fun.

The next day we opened presents at Nancy's parents' house, with a lot of relatives and friends in attendance. Then we were packing three seventy-pound boxes, right at the baggage size and weight limit, because I was flying back to the Virgin Islands that evening. We packed all those sheets and towels, small carpets, appliances, bar guides and cookbooks, everything we'd need for charter. Nancy would be flying a day later and also bringing three boxes.

A MILE DOWN

• • •

Our guests for the first charter had written on their preference sheets from the broker, "We are heavy drinkers." They had a list of ten or fifteen special mixed drinks they wanted in quantity, so we bought liquor at four different shops (to find specialty items such as Grey Goose Orange) and groceries from more than half a dozen stores. Eleven adults plus four crew for five days. We were grateful to have charters. Most boats were having a lousy year because of the recession. We were the rising stars, the new boat with no direct competition because of the number of staterooms. It was gratifying to see all of my hassles in Turkey, Spain, Gibraltar, and Trinidad finally paying off.

This first charter group was easy, which was good because we didn't do everything perfectly. I wasn't really a bartender yet, so Bobby, the man who was paying for the charter and had invited his friends to help him celebrate his fiftieth birthday, made the drinks with great flair. I kept the bottles and ice and glasses coming and watched closely. Captains are expected to be good bartenders.

We also had a rigging problem, and again the guests were gracious. We had a lovely sail one morning across the channel on a beam reach from the Baths to Marina Cay, but when it came time to furl the sail, there was a lot of resistance. During the paint job, we had removed the headstay and let it hang to the side, and apparently this had broken one of the connections. It had been hidden by the sail wrapped around it, so the problem had not been visible, and we hadn't tested the sail on our way from Trinidad because we had only motored. I couldn't repair it now, with the sail out, underway, and guests aboard, and I was worried that we wouldn't get the sail furled or that we might rip it.

As I was distracted by this, standing above the winch to look over the pilothouse at the foil, holding the line in my left hand, a large gust of wind filled the sail, and the line, which I was holding too high above the winch, came free. I grabbed for it, instinctively, but this was not a good instinct, especially

189

while wearing fingerless gloves. The rope burn across four fingers of my left hand was extreme. Only a few patches of skin were completely missing down to bleeding, exposed flesh, but all four fingers looked like deformed wax. They were white, especially after I dunked my hand into a bucket of ice, and the pain was intense. I did get the sail furled, and brought us safely into an anchorage, but that was all I could do. I felt awful for the guests. It was a putzy bit of sailing we had just done.

By the end of the five-day charter, my fingers were healing, despite my fears that they'd be permanently deformed, and the trip was considered a great success. Bobby gave us a $2,000 tip, wrote us a lovely card, and gave glowing reviews to the broker, who sent a note of praise to the clearinghouse, who then passed the note on to other brokers. I was embarrassed about our problems with the roller furling, but we were well on our way to a successful business.

There had been one small conversation with Bobby, however, that I would never forget. It was late in the trip, after he had asked about my business and plans, and he was wishing me well. He was a handsome man, likeable in every way, and he meant only the best, didn't mean to insult me, certainly, but he said, comparing my desires to succeed in this business to his own desires years before as he was starting his own business, "I know what it's like. You're nobody, and you want to become somebody."

This comment made sense in terms of the business. It was a new business, even if it was my second go and I had already run years of great charters, set up a unique educational program through Stanford, raised over $600,000 in private loans, completed the construction of a boat in Turkey, rescued another boat from Mexico, managed to get the Turkish boat back after bankruptcy, and crossed oceans umpteen times. It was true that I hadn't made a lot of money yet, even to pay off my debts, and that I was new to the brokered charter industry. But he wasn't talking only about the business, he was talking about me, about who I was, about my worth as a person. And I objected to being limited to this business and this role as captain. I had taught at Stanford and Cornell. I had been published in the *Atlantic Monthly,* one of my stories printed and reprinted in half a million copies around the world.

I didn't share these thoughts with Bobby, of course. But I realized that even if I succeeded wildly in this business, with all my debts paid off and bringing in $300,000 a year, or even building a fleet of boats and bringing in millions a year, it still fundamentally wouldn't mean anything to me except financial freedom. It wasn't how I measured who I was, and it never would be. I would always feel somewhat alienated in this role of captain or small business owner. I was a writer and a teacher. That's who I was. I needed to start writing again soon.

The second charter was easy, a fun ten days. I practiced my skills as a bartender, enjoying it, and the kids performed skits at night on the large aft deck area, their parents lounging on the cushioned poop deck. Everyone called me "Captain Dave." It didn't feel like a job at all.

Immediately after this charter, however, when we went into the clearinghouse office in Roadtown to pick up our mail and news, we learned that a hurricane was headed our way. It would probably pass south of us, but it could swing north.

This presented an uncomfortable situation. We were too late to run away from it, and we didn't have good options for weathering a hurricane in the Virgin Islands.

I finally decided to anchor in North Sound on Virgin Gorda. The sound is expansive and almost fully enclosed, like a big lake, most of it forty-five to sixty feet deep. We'd be completely exposed to wind, but we could drag on our anchor all over that bay and not hit anything.

As it turned out, the hurricane tracked far south of us and we never had wind more than thirty knots. We would have been fine anywhere in the Virgin Islands. But the experience drove home the fact that we were exposed up here during hurricane season. Nancy and I talked it over and decided to head south. We would island-hop through the Antilles for a month, spend another month in Trinidad working, then sail back up in time for the November charter shows. We had wanted to take a break and relax in the Virgin Islands for these months, but worrying about hurricanes did not promise to be very relaxing.

We returned to Roadtown to make some arrangements and take on food, water, and diesel, then sailed for Nevis, our first stop. It would be the longest leg, about eighteen hours. We passed between Peter Island and Dead Chest Island just after sunset and were blasted by thirty knots of wind, heavy rain, and swells about twelve feet, leftovers from the hurricane that had passed farther south. If we continued on to Nevis, we'd be pounding directly into this the entire time.

I decided this suffering was pointless. We weren't on a schedule. I turned around and anchored for the night in Great Harbour. We left at noon the next day, the conditions much improved, and made Nevis the next morning. A spectacular volcanic mountain rising from the water, its slopes dense jungle. We anchored in light blue water just down from the Four Seasons. Our view was of undeveloped beach, then several miles of palm trees, then jungle leading up to volcanic cone. It was our honeymoon, finally.

We zipped ashore in our new dinghy and walked a few boardwalks to have ice cream and window shop. Then a driver took Nancy and Stephen and me halfway around the island, showing us landmarks, monkeys, mangoes, and jungle. We stopped at several plantations that are now bed and breakfasts. Nancy and I fell in love, at least for the day, with gingerbread architecture.

Late that afternoon, after we had changed at the boat, Stephen dropped us off on the beach with the dinghy and we walked into the Four Seasons. We joined the other honeymooners in the pools and hot tubs and took in the gorgeous sunset. It was one of our favorite things to do, crashing resorts, and this was a coup.

The next day we cruised the western shores of Dominica and Guadeloupe (lovely as long as we didn't look too closely), and then it was on to Martinique and St. Lucia. Stephen left us to fly home to Trinidad, as planned, and we found out we had a new charter from Ed Hamilton, the most important broker in the market. If we ran a good charter for Ed, we were set. We would fill our twenty weeks every year with no problem. And it was a short, easy charter, for the Young Presidents' Association. Ed didn't tell us who the group of ten men were, but we knew, and we felt flattered they had picked us over the $7 million, 85-foot performance catamaran they had been on the year before. The charter was coming up soon, at the end of October, just before the charter show, and we were looking forward to it.

We were also enjoying our honeymoon on St. Lucia. We spent almost a week there, just taking a break. I began writing, for two hours every morning, for the first time in five years. I started with a pirate novel but quickly set it aside and began this memoir. It would be titled *The Afterlife of Ruin,* about how everything had worked out after it had seemed all was lost. A story of the American Dream. It would also be about how my father hadn't been able to see the possibility of continuing on in some new way, and about finally escaping his legacy, after ten years of insomnia and fifteen years of being fairly sure I was doomed to kill myself. It wouldn't get bogged down in too much about my father, and it would be fundamentally hopeful and cheery, unlike my previous book, which every agent had said lacked redemption and was too depressing. This one wouldn't be fancy, either, just an easy read.

After writing each morning, I had lunch with Nancy and we zipped off in our dinghy to enjoy the beach or snorkeling or hiking, or we'd just kayak from the boat. Nancy went back to her days of floating on air mattresses, a skill she had first perfected along the Turkish Coast. At sunset we'd be on the aft deck with an alcoholic concoction, usually involving ice cream, or in the pool or hot tub of the resort.

We talked a lot about our future together. We were in love, and not just with each other. Our yacht was a spectacular home, a stand-out in every harbor, and the Caribbean is a beautiful place. But what we loved most was our freedom. We would work no more than twenty weeks per year, and we would have the rest of the year to do anything we wanted. Travel was high on our list. We would see most of the world. But we were surprised at the other things.

I wanted to go back to the university, for instance. Being a captain and running a business lacked dignity and engagement, I had realized, even if I made a lot of money. "And we don't have any friends out here," I told Nancy. "And it's not as if there are great literary gatherings on St. Lucia."

"You should do it," she said. "Become a medievalist. And keep writing every day, too. It's all you've talked about the whole time I've known you, even though you haven't written a word until now. Mr. Big Mouth."

"Thanks."

"If we decide to spend more time back in the Bay Area, I'm going to one of the dance places—maybe the Metronome—to take their instructor series. Or culinary school. I'm not sure. Maybe both."

"Freedom is what it's about," I said. "Hand over the boat to a few crew and not even work the twenty weeks. A PhD or ballroom dance or just cruise around the Med in a little powerboat, go up all the canals through France."

"Italy," Nancy said. "More time in Italy."

"Well, the sun's down. Off to the hot tub?"

"How about something with Midori first?"

Praising one's time in the islands always has to come with a warning, however. Every day at least one or two and sometimes as many as five different local guys came by in their little boats to sell food and trinkets. I finally tried to save one of them the wasted effort. He had a boat that looked like a grass hut, with banana leaves up the side and on the roof. He was the most enterprising of them all.

"I feel bad that you keep spending the gas to come out here," I told him honestly. I was leaning on the wide, varnished rail that came up about three feet off our aft deck. He was ten feet below me, peering up through the fronds. "Really, we're never going to buy anything."

"You never gonna buy?"

"That's right," I said.

"You got to eat," he said. "Where you get your food?"

"We're already fully stocked. We stock up at supermarkets, to save money."

"You got money to buy a gift for your wife."

"No, I don't. I really don't. I know you're not going to believe me, because no one here ever believes me once they see the boat, but I really don't have any extra cash right now."

"I know you got cash. I know the owner of this big boat give you cash."

"I'm the owner," I said. "And I don't have cash. This boat is a business. We're just starting up. So we had to put a lot of money into it, but we haven't gotten any money out of it yet." I was giving this random man a ridiculous amount of my personal information, but I was tired of our shitty interactions.

"You not the owner," he told me finally.

"I'm the owner."

"You not the owner." And then he started his outboard again and turned his boat around to leave. He smiled up at me and waved one finger in the air. "You not the owner. That not your boat."

"Fuck off," I said, and he just laughed as he putted away.

I stormed back into the pilothouse, where Nancy was sitting and had been listening.

"There's no way to get along," she said. "Unless we just hand them money for nothing every day. That's the only way we can have peace, and even that's not peace, because then they want to sell us more."

"There is the whole history of the slave trade," I said. "And I guess we look like the latest wave in colonization. And really we are. We're using their home for our own economic gain through selling charters, and we're not sharing the profits with them. It's still the first world taking away their wealth."

"But it still sucks," she said, and I had to agree. There is just no way around differences in wealth, even apparent wealth. Money rules us all.

On our way down the west coast of St. Lucia the next day, before crossing to St. Vincent, we cruised in close to the Pitons, which are truly magnificent: two very sharp, green, volcanic mountains rising thousands of feet straight from the water's edge. It's probably one of the most spectacular views in the world, with a lovely bay at the Pitons' feet and palm trees all along the shoreline.

Our next stop was Bequia, just south of St. Vincent, the beginning of the Grenadines. Nancy and I loved Bequia. A friendly town with flowers lining the walkways, an abundance of bookstores and restaurants, beautiful beaches. It was a place to rest, a perfect place for a honeymoon. We stayed for almost a week.

From Bequia we worked our way through the rest of the Grenadines. Our favorites were the Tobago Cays. An enormous horseshoe-shaped reef several miles long and fifty yards wide protecting three tiny islands with perfect beaches. The snorkeling was by far the best we'd ever experienced, rated as one of the top three sites in the world. Clean, clear water, bright sun, and miles of living coral reef in every color with thousands of fish. We followed whole schools, saw new species, felt the warm water on our skin, the light current and waves rocking us gently. I've loved tropical fish all my life, at one point in junior high had eight aquariums spread throughout the house. For years, even in upstate New York, in grad school, I had gazed at fish every night, watched how they fluttered, imagined myself suspended in warm water with them, so this was heaven for me, to spend a little quality time with the fish.

On September 14 we reached Grenada, our jumping-off point for the final passage to Trinidad. We went to an Internet café to check e-mail for the first time in over a week and saw news on Yahoo that was difficult to believe. Terrorists flying passenger planes into the twin towers in New York. We felt extremely disconnected, finding out about this event three days late. On the television in the café, leaders from all the Caribbean countries were condemning the attacks and offering their sadness and support to the United States.

We sailed early the next morning for Trinidad and arrived just before dark. Back in the ugly industrial port, but this time we wouldn't have to haul out, and I would take some time to write every day. We wouldn't repeat the panic of our first visit to Trinidad.

It was good to see Stephen again. He and two friends put another coat of varnish on the exterior wood, polished the hull, sanded the deck, and sanded and varnished every stateroom and the main salon and all the floors throughout the boat. They also sanded and painted the engine room and the two largest bilge areas. They even sanded and painted the insides of my two water tanks, which was an especially nasty job. I bought a thick epoxy paint, high in solids, and a big fan to pull out the fumes. The guys wore respirators, but it was still a tough job.

The most difficult job, however, was repainting all eight guest bathrooms. The white epoxy paint over the steel had started to bubble from moisture. Stephen pointed out that this should never have happened, that the painters in Turkey had not used the correct primer. By now, he had zero respect for the Turks. He and his friends went through each bathroom, first sanding down to steel with a big orbital sander and forty-grit paper. Then they worked up through layers of primer and filler and paint and finer sandings to a finish that looked great and would last. But it was a huge amount of work, more than any of us had expected.

"Next summer, someone else can paint your other tanks," Stephen told me. "I not doing no more inside painting on this boat, boy."

"You can just supervise next summer," I told him. "We'll leave the boat with you, and you can hire others to do the work."

"I doesn't mind the outside painting, or the outside varnish," he said. "Just no more inside, boy."

I was already leaving most of the work to Stephen's supervision. He always worked hard, whether I was there or not, and he knew far more about painting and varnishing than I did. I was focusing on the rigging, systems maintenance, my writing, and running the business.

By the time we left Trinidad the second time, we were happy to get out of there. The boat looked perfect inside and out, thanks to Stephen, and we wouldn't have to return until next summer.

We cleared customs on Friday, again with the man with long purple nails, who this time could not find any reason to detain us, and we spent the remainder of the afternoon and evening stowing and checking everything. We tightened the standing rigging and checked our electronics and engines and tanks and the weather, and we went to bed early so we'd be well rested, since it would be just the two of us doing alternating ninety-minute watches for three days.

WE LEFT AT 7 A.M., found the seas very light once we were out of the dragon's mouth, and had an entirely pleasant first day and night, as predicted on the weather report. We napped and ate and read, and I checked the systems after every watch. It was good to be on our way, looking forward to a successful winter in the Virgin Islands.

The next day, Sunday, the waves were two to three feet but glassy and reflective. The surface, untouched by any wind, made the ocean seem solid rather than liquid, a bright metal sheet crumpling without sound. This was unusual, and I stood at the aft of the pilothouse wondering at it. In the distance ahead we could see a small squall, a cloud with dark rain beneath it and the waters roughened. Nancy was happy to see this. It would dump a little rain and cool us off a bit. Then the sky would brighten again and the sun would steam the water off the deck.

But this squall didn't pass so quickly. For almost an hour, we had thick rain and gusty winds, the seas increasing. I was listening to music on a Walkman and enjoying the occasional spray and the feel of powering through the waves. I liked this, the raw animal nature of the boat. The growling of the big Perkins diesels.

It was late afternoon, less than an hour before dark, and within just a few minutes the spray was coming over the deck with every wave, and then I could hear howling in the rigging and my wind instruments showed thirty to thirty-five knots. I took the headphones off and listened more carefully to the wind, the engines, and the other sounds of the boat, the various things shifting as we hit a bigger wave and rolled about twenty-five degrees.

In only another couple of minutes, the sea changed yet again, building far too quickly into forty-knot winds pushing up larger swells, and the wind was coming from too close to north. We weren't in gusty tradewinds or squall winds anymore. We were in something with a counterclockwise, cyclonic movement. There had been nothing at all on the Inmarsat-C weather forecast.

I called on the radio for weather info. "U.S. Coast Guard, U.S. Coast Guard, U.S. Coast Guard, this is the sailing vessel *Bird of Paradise.*"

No response. We were a hundred miles from any land except Aves Island, which is only a small spit of sand sticking up absurdly in the middle of the Caribbean Sea.

"Calling all stations," I repeated three times, and again no response.

Only a few minutes had passed, but the swells had become streaky white with foam and were breaking and confused, coming from two different headings, the newer storm waves from the north colliding with swells from the east. Our heading was impossible, since it put us in the trough of swells that were big enough now to make us roll fifty degrees on our side. I changed our heading to go into them and throttled down because the bow was hitting so hard as we raised up over one wave and slammed into the next.

The acceleration of conditions was astounding. Fifty knots on the wind gauge, and in the dim light, the white of waves breaking. Waves five times the size of what we'd had only an hour earlier—steep, close together, not in long organized lines from one direction but hunching up in individual hills and peaks. I throttled down again, making only five knots and still slamming hard, solid water coming over our bow, the bowsprit buried each time.

The light was dying, and I had to lean forward to read my wind gauge. It showed fifty-eight knots, which is storm force 11, right before a hurricane. I didn't know what I was going into. If it was a hurricane, running would be the only option because the winds could be anything, 100 or 160 miles per hour or even higher. If it was a low-pressure storm that had come from north of us, however, or a white squall kicked up suddenly from colliding weather systems, it would be wiser to cut straight through, exposing us to risk for a shorter time and keeping our defensive position of bow first, so we wouldn't roll over in a trough.

Nancy was already below in the main salon looking on the Inmarsat for any new weather reports, and we did receive a new report but it said nothing at all about this storm. Absolutely no mention. According to the Tropical Prediction Center in Miami, Florida, we were experiencing no more than twenty knots of wind and eight- or nine-foot swells, normal conditions.

I tried the VHF again. Tried calling the U.S. Coast Guard, tried calling the French Navy, tried calling in Spanish, tried calling all stations. There was no response. So I decided to give a report to the Coast Guard in case they could hear me even though I couldn't hear them.

"U.S. Coast Guard, U.S. Coast Guard, this is the sailing vessel *Bird of Paradise,* the sailing vessel *Bird of Paradise.* We are at latitude 15 degrees 22.5 minutes north, longitude 63 degrees 27.6 minutes west. We are in 60-knot winds and seas over 30 feet. We are bearing zero one five degrees northeast at—" But then, in the last light of day, we saw an enormous wave. Our bow went up and still the wave rose and then it was breaking above us. Our bow went so high, so straight up into the air for so long, we could feel our entire yacht—all 200,000 pounds of it—actually hanging, ready to fall backward off the wave, and still the wave rose higher and the part that had broken was blown over our pilothouse at highway speed, thousands of gallons of water turned into smoke.

We hung and the boat fell to the side, everything crashing. I could hear our wedding gifts, which had been stored in cupboards in the galley, hitting the cabinet doors so hard they broke open and everything fell twenty feet across the main salon to the port side. Other heavy thuds and bangs throughout the boat, things breaking. And then our bow plowed into the next wave with such force that our teak platform on the steel bowsprit was blown off its bolts. Our bow went deep into solid water, and that wave turned us ninety degrees. We tipped left in the trough, broadside now to the waves, and the next wave hit the side of our hull so hard we were picked up out of the water and dropped again. Everything from the main salon crashed back into the galley.

I gunned the engines and brought us around to port, spinning the spoked wooden helm a full eleven turns, so that we took the next wave on the bow, though I was worried about the integrity of the bow. What was left of the heavy teak platform and its stainless steel railing was loose and banging. I was afraid the force of that wood flying up would catch the underside of our roller furler and break our headstay. If that happened, our heavy wooden masts could come down backward right on top of us.

These were the worst seas I had ever been in. It was likely we would lose our lives. No help was available, and the conditions were so bad we wouldn't be able to get into our life raft.

Nancy remained calm. She helped assess the damage. "Everything from under the stern platform is out on deck.

Both dinghies still attached. Galley, everything has opened and fallen. Do you want me to check more below?"

A lot of hard objects were flying back and forth across the main salon, but our Inmarsat station was down there and we needed weather information. "We have to find out what we're in. It could be a hurricane, but I don't think it is, because it couldn't have formed so fast and it feels too cold. I think it has to be a cold storm from north of us that collided with a tropical system."

Nancy went below to the chart table.

"Tell them we have more than sixty knots of wind," I yelled. The storm and engines were very loud. "Seas over thirty feet, with some bigger waves mixed in, and no report for this area. Tell them please send a report. And be careful. Hold on."

It was dark now. I couldn't see the bowsprit anymore, but I could see the steaming light halfway up our mainmast lighting the headstay, which was swinging wildly back and forth, several feet to either side. I was afraid it would go. After each concussion, I looked up to check.

I couldn't see the waves now, couldn't see what was coming. I focused on the compass, keeping us on a heading between zero and thirty degrees, using more throttle on the engines whenever we threatened to fall off course. The wind was so loud I kept thinking I was hearing things: other boats, whistling in our engines, Nancy's voice, songs as if a radio were playing, though I had turned off the Walkman. Nancy said she thought she could hear songs, too, now and then.

There was no predicting when the hardest hits would come. But it was never more than five or ten seconds before another wave would stop our bow and the shock would reverberate through the boat. Then solid water would crash over the foredeck, the windows underwater, then clear except for spray that pelted them in flurries.

I was beyond caring about the wedding gifts and equipment and other things that were being destroyed. We had worked hard to prepare for our charter, and the boat had looked beautiful only the day before, and this damage would set us back, but all I wanted was for us to survive. For that to happen, the headstay needed to remain attached, the rudder and steering had to hold, and the engines needed to keep running. And I had to keep us from getting rolled over and buried.

The experience felt similar, in its grimness, to the time I had steered with only the engines and no rudder for ten hours off the Moroccan coast. But these seas were far worse. Even with a working rudder, these were more dangerous because they were so sharp and irregular. They were straight walls, some of them, with water breaking down onto us, and each one hit us from a different angle. I steered into them for hours, not able to see but trying to guess where they were. Everything done by feel and by the compass. Nancy stopped trying to go below or to tie anything down and we just braced ourselves and waited. I found myself saying, "Please, please," over and over in my head, though I'm not religious and don't pray. It's impossible not to beg for help, even if you have no one to beg.

I wanted it to end, but it went on for a long time, about six hours. Living second by second in darkness and fear makes six hours an exquisitely long time.

But the wind and waves did finally die down, to 40 knots and 15 feet, then 30–35 knots and 10 or 12 feet, and finally 25 knots and 10 or 12 feet, which was manageable. It was near midnight when I asked Nancy to take the helm for an hour so I could inspect the boat and take a nap.

In the engine room, I found water and sediment in the diesel filters. Water is deadly to a diesel engine. If the water filled these and the other filters and made it to the injectors, the engines would stop.

The steel walls between the diesel and wastewater tanks must have ruptured from the force of the waves. This was unheard of, but it must have happened to both tanks because they were isolated from each other by valves and yet both had taken in water and sediment. We had been hit hard.

I turned off the port engine, bled water and sediment from its tank and then its filter, and restarted it, then repeated for the other engine. I was drenched in sweat and dizzy from all the diesel fumes, naked except for my shorts, with diesel on my hands and feet. I climbed back up to the helm and turned on the starboard engine. It raced and fell a bit but held.

"There's so much crap in them right now," I told Nancy. "So much that must be getting through those dirty filters. Especially the starboard engine, since I did it last. I should probably bleed it underway, to try to blow some of the crap out of the injectors."

I went below again and stood over the starboard diesel loosening and retightening the caps on each injector, one at a time. The engine could run temporarily on just five cylinders instead of its full six. When uncovered, the injectors spat out diesel mist at high pressure, covering me head to toe, but they also spat out some bubbles, which were air, and I saw round clear drops of water slide down the side of the engine like fat.

The only thing I wanted now was sleep. We had been underway for almost two days, just the two of us alternating at the helm, ninety minutes each, and then I had taken the helm for six hours in the storm. But there were more problems before I could rest.

In the aft bilge, water was rushing from side to side like a river as we rolled in the waves, hitting the underside of the aft stateroom floors with such force it was coming up along the walls, in every small carpenter's gap. The mahogany was swollen and was going to warp.

I opened the small hatch for the bilge. The water ran unchecked now, over both varnished floors, back and forth from one room to the other as we rolled. I grabbed a small plastic bucket, opened a porthole, and started bailing.

On one bailing trip, as I took the few steps from the bilge

toward the porthole with my full bucket, we hit a large wave and I slipped on the wet varnished floor and went straight up. I was about five feet off the floor, horizontal in the air, holding the bucket of water. Then gravity kicked in and I was dropped on my back onto the wood and the bucket.

I couldn't move, couldn't breathe. The boat was still rocking and bucking, the water running back and forth, hitting the underside of the floor hard and sloshing me from above, and I was sliding around, my head hitting against the foot of the bed.

Then I took a breath, which hurt. My back was stunned. I managed to sit up and breathe again, fell sideways, then sat up and held on. I waited a few minutes, thinking that if I had cracked my head open and were bleeding and unconscious, Nancy wouldn't even know, and in these conditions, without an autopilot, she wouldn't be able to leave the helm. We were taking such stupid risks. What was I doing, bailing at night on a varnished floor in big seas when I was dizzy, exhausted, and nearly naked?

When I was able, I made my way slowly down the hall and up to the pilothouse to tell Nancy what had happened. She looked at my back. "You took off some of the skin by your scar," she said. "And it's red. You hit the entire muscle on your right side."

I lay down on the pilothouse cushions, our bed for the past two days, and tried to breathe. My back was so tight, it wasn't easy.

"This boat isn't worth it," I said. "It's not worth dying or even getting hurt out here."

"I don't want to do this ever again," Nancy said. "Next time we have to stop at Rodney Bay so we're always close to islands, instead of a hundred miles from land."

"I agree," I said. She had managed to stay calm through all of it, which was impressive. And she was still willing to do these delivery trips, just closer to land.

By daybreak, the conditions had died down to twenty knots and ten feet, but the seas looked cold, as if we were much farther north, the seas I knew from Alaska and off the Washington and Oregon coasts. Maybe it was the clouds everywhere in the distance, and the sky that was hazy and white, so that water, clouds, and sky all shared the same color, all seemed part of the same body. I remembered this same seascape on a morning on *Grendel,* leaving Victoria; I remembered it outside of Ketchikan with my father; I remembered it on a purse seiner in the Cook Inlet. But it was strange for the Caribbean.

Out of the milky white came a large container ship, the *Tropic Sun.* It passed us to starboard, heading southeast. I hailed the captain on the VHF, asking for weather information.

"We didn't have any warning," he said. "We had about the same conditions as you, though much farther north. Nothing on any forecast or report."

I asked what we could expect ahead, on our way to the Virgin Islands.

"All conditions diminishing, it seems. Though there's still no report."

"Have you ever seen the reporting stations fail like this?" I asked.

"No," he said.

I thanked him and continued on toward a far line of thick clouds, hoping we weren't heading straight into another storm. The strange weather was everywhere, land was far away, and there were no reports, so there was nothing to do but just continue on and hope for the best.

Later that morning, the wind came up to more than thirty knots and the seas built. I began to have trouble holding my course on the compass. I had the helm all the way to port, but I couldn't turn.

"Can you take the helm?" I asked Nancy. "I need to check the hydraulics."

"Oh great," she said.

"Yeah, wouldn't it be nice if the rudder had a problem again? Give me a minute, then turn the helm slowly all the way to one side, then all the way to the other, then five and a half turns to the middle."

I made my way carefully to the aft staterooms. The water rushed back and forth over the floor. I had to take care of that, had to get the 220-volt submersible pump. But for now I needed to focus on the steering. I pulled up the mattress in one of the aft staterooms to inspect the big white hydraulic pump, its solid stainless ram gliding forward, pushing the fitting that turned the rudder post. Everything was working smoothly, no signs of breakage or failure or slipping.

The problem had to be with the rudder itself, which I had no way of inspecting. When I retook the helm I slowed the engines and turned all the way to starboard in a circle, which worked fine. Then I tried turning a circle to port, and this worked fine on certain headings but not toward the course we wanted. The rudder could do what should have been difficult, but it could not do what should have been easy. I could not imagine what sort of damage would accomplish that. It's a fairly simple thing, a rudder. Just a shaft, a big piece of metal hanging aft of it, and a skeg forward for support. But this rudder was acting in mysterious ways.

"We have some kind of damage," I told Nancy. "And there's also the problem with the diesel tanks, and the aft bilge water. We probably shouldn't just go wherever the rudder will take us. The problems could get worse."

"I can't believe this," she said. "Didn't we already have the rudder problem, and didn't we already replace it with a new rudder?" She turned away and shook her head.

"We don't have any money," I said. "But there's a $16,500 hull deductible on the policy. So we have to figure out something. A free tow from the Coast Guard, then maybe the lenders for the repairs. God, it makes my head hurt."

"We were supposed to be past this kind of problem," Nancy said.

So I called the Coast Guard. It was hard to believe I was calling again for assistance due to a disabled rudder. It did not seem possible to be having this same problem again. I really felt like Oedipus trying to run from his fate. Different ocean, different year, different business plan, different rudder even, but the same problem, possibly with the same ruinous consequences.

When the Coast Guard cutter arrived, it was dusk. After a fairly calm, light afternoon, full of sunshine and hope, the wind was back up to over thirty and the waves were increasing, just in time for our work on deck.

This cutter represented the cream of the U.S. Coast Guard. A fast boat for drug interdiction in their most active waters. It would be a crack crew onboard. The captain sounded cheerful and confident, and he spent a full hour planning how we would do this tow, then he took a practice pass, which took another hour.

When he began his real pass, finally, from half a mile away, Nancy and I walked forward to the bow. I had the engines in neutral, our boat dead in the water and rocking hideously broadside to the seas, as requested, so that the cutter would have the privileged position of heading into the waves. It was cold in the wind and rain and spray.

"Let's do it right," I said. "Let's catch the damn thing, pull it in, and get it over the windlass. One time."

As their boat came closer, we could hear the big engines. They were staying mostly in neutral, engaging only periodically in short bursts of power. They had a spotlight on us and all their lights on. They seemed sleek but not quite in control.

The guys on the aft deck were shouting orders at each other and struggling to keep their footing. Three of them had throwing lines with green glow sticks attached, and a spotter in front was going to say when to throw.

"Not yet, not yet," he was yelling, and others were yelling, too. They were making it seem much more exciting and complicated than it really needed to be. Nancy and I were just waiting quietly at the lifelines for them to throw.

More yelling, and finally the green light stick came arcing toward us through the rain. Nancy caught it, mostly with her face but also with her arms, and we led it outside our lifelines and stanchions, through the scupper, then pulled in an incredibly long heaving line before we finally reached the loop of the towline.

The cutter was coming closer. Their stern was swinging toward us, the driver still using his engines only in short bursts. The guys on the aft deck yelled at him to go, go, go, forward, forward, but it was too late. Their starboard stern rose up on a wave and bashed the end of our bowsprit, an explosion of steel on steel and some other fragile object on their boat, a light or something, shattering. Then the driver gunned it fast away from us, and they all yelled to slow down, slow down, because we were holding the end of their towline. I was afraid we might be yanked overboard or have our limbs torn off, but we just pulled the heavy wet loop as fast as we could over our windlass. I checked that it wasn't caught on anything, then signaled with my arms in the air that we were done and told Nancy we should get away from the bow in case the line snapped or the windlass went flying off its mounts.

We hurried back to the pilothouse and I called the captain on the radio, letting him know our end was ready. Neither of us mentioned the collision.

He let out line for a while, getting farther away from us, then caught up the slack and pulled us with a jerk, our bow tipping sideways and coming around fast in an extreme yaw to port then back to starboard. We kept going to starboard, like a waterskier going for outside the wake, leaning away from the tow boat, and I tried to correct with port rudder, which had some effect but not much. The cutter's solution was to speed up, which seemed to me a dubious solution. We whipped back and forth but mostly to starboard, and the captain said he was letting out more line, finding the proper tow length so we'd be in sync on the swells, and the tow did become a bit smoother, if too fast for my tastes, but then the line broke.

Their boat receded, we slowed, and I called on the radio to notify them. We were in a heavy squall, over forty knots of wind blowing buckets of rain into our pilothouse from behind, so that even twenty feet into the pilothouse, the ceiling was wet. The rain was cold, too. This was definitely a northern storm that had come down into the Caribbean. I went forward on deck and pulled up their towline, about fifty feet, which meant it hadn't been severed by any chafing on our end.

I stood there for a while staring absentmindedly at the green light shining through the messy pile of their heaving line. I was drenched in the rain, and only my hand on a stanchion was keeping me from being thrown overboard. We would have to catch their line again. I wanted to sleep. I wondered why I persisted in this whole boating thing.

One thing about being at sea is that you don't really get to stop. You can never say, "Okay, to hell with this, I've had enough, I'm outta here." Until you arrive in port, you're stuck, and conditions can always worsen, the boat can always break in new ways, whether you're prepared or not. Even in port, you can slip anchor, blow against other anchored boats in crosswinds and currents, or run aground. In a marina, battering, chafing, and electrolysis are still possible, as are propane explosion, electrical fire, sinking through siphoning and all the hazards of docking, all the expensive things you can run into and crush. A boat simply does not allow for genuine rest. Its essential nature is peril, held in check only through enormous effort and expense.

I had worked hard to get this boat back after the bankruptcy, and that effort seemed odd to me now. How had I believed that it would not be the same horrific shit over and over if I got back on board? What was wrong with me?

THE CAPTAIN OF the cutter said his crew had tied something incorrectly. Apparently this fifty feet of line I now had on deck had been tied to a longer piece. I said no problem and waited, hoping they'd figure out how to tie a bowline, but they were out there for quite a while and didn't return, so I called again on the radio.

"We dropped something in the water," the captain said. "And it looks like we need to retrieve it. We'll be back in just a minute."

So Nancy and I waited, curious to find out what they had dropped. We could see them circling around in the rain, and something flashing in the water. Then they seemed to give up. We could still see the flashing.

When the captain came back on the radio, he sounded very calm, as if dropping something in the water and not recovering it were a regular occurrence. He suggested we try the tow from starboard this time, to prevent such extreme yawing. He also wanted to try the approach from upwind, coming down past us, which sounded bizarre to me, but I didn't feel I could object. I was supposed to leave my boat dead in the troughs again, so it was up to him, whatever he wanted to do, and he had already run into us once, so somehow that seemed to take the worry out of it.

Nancy and I returned to the bow. The cutter was being blown down onto us, its stern sagging, which seemed inevitable and was the reason I wouldn't have tried from upwind. The captain had to punch the engines to bring his bow around and avoid hitting us again, which put him past us, but his crew threw two lines anyway, into the water. Then he was in reverse, trying to get back, which was not going to work in these waves. Luckily, his crew decided to throw the last line. The thrower did an amazing job, from the distance he was at, and we caught it, led it through the scupper, and hauled in until we had the loop over our windlass.

Back in the pilothouse, I told the captain we were ready and neither of us mentioned that we were towing from the port side again instead of the starboard side. Then Nancy yelled for me and I went aft. She pointed overboard. There was a white canister life raft floating near us. I looked up on our pilothouse roof at our own life raft to confirm that it wasn't ours.

"That must have been what they dropped in the water," Nancy said. She had one hand over her nose and mouth, which is what she does when she's laughing so hard she's starting to snort. I laughed, too. It was pretty incredible. They had somehow dropped their life raft overboard and then hadn't been able to retrieve it. And the life raft hadn't deployed, either. It should have automatically inflated.

Nancy and I checked the towline every thirty minutes and finally asked for slack to adjust the line. It was chafing in several places. The cutter wasn't careful to stay in front of our bow, however. The new helmsman (the captain had retired for the evening) managed to get his boat behind our boat, facing the opposite direction. We're facing one way, with the towline going back underneath our boat, and he's a hundred yards off our stern facing the other way. How he managed to think this was okay was beyond me. I explained the situation to him, then gave Nancy the radio and went aft with a flashlight. As he pulled us backward through the water, I could see the towline coming out from under our stern on the starboard side, shallow and bent at an angle, which meant it was hung up on something, probably our damaged rudder. I let out a little yell of frustration, and Nancy wanted to know what was up.

"Tell him the towline is caught on our rudder and to quit pulling us backward," I yelled.

Nancy told him this over the radio, but he kept pulling us backward.

I went to the radio. "Look," I told him, "you can't keep towing us backward with the towline caught around our rudder."

"Roger that, sir, we're trying to address the problem now."

"Maybe you could let the line sink, pull in some slack, then use the slack to make a turn to port. Hopefully the line will clear."

I could hear his engines. He was still trying to pull his way out of it, which was impossible. I didn't want to think uncharitable thoughts about our rescuers, but this helmsman had zero idea how to drive a boat.

"You might consider letting the line sag and sink first," I said. "My wife will be on the radio, and I'll be on the stern letting her know where the line is."

"Roger that."

I couldn't help making a comment to Nancy. "If he'd pulled a water-skier even once in his life, he'd know how not to get the line all screwed up."

"Maybe it's his first time out," Nancy said.

I went back to the stern and gave reports to Nancy, which she passed on to the helmsman. He finally let us drift and the line sag until I couldn't see it anymore. Then he drove a bit, but still going the opposite way, not trying to turn. The line came up and I saw that it was on our starboard side now, the same side as the cutter. If he went now toward our bow, the line would clear.

"Tell him to turn hard to port."

Nancy relayed the message, but we were drifting over the line. It would go back under us again. Then he gunned his engines, still going in the opposite direction. He was not trying to turn to port at all. He was just going to yank us around from behind at full speed.

"Hold on!" I yelled to Nancy. "We might capsize."

Our boat yanked suddenly to starboard, tipping over, and I heard a ripping sound of the line coming up through the water, then whacking the side of our ninety-foot hull like a piano string. We went fast backward and sideways through the water, I fell down on the deck, grabbed on to the kayak that was tied, and then we went level again, the bow flung around and yanked forward.

"Holy shit," Nancy said.

I got back up and joined her at the helm. I called the cutter on the radio. "We're okay, I think," I said. "And the line's clear. But that was dangerous and ridiculous. That was the closest I've ever come to capsizing."

No response. So we waited. Then, finally, "Roger that. Line is clear." Then he asked that we not stop again for chafing. He said he preferred to take the chance of it severing. So I said fine and went to drain the diesel tanks and pump the aft bilge.

After pumping the aft bilge, I used my flashlight to examine the area, as I had several other times, and this time I found a hairline crack, an actual crack in our hull. It was about six inches long, a foot forward of the rudder stock and slightly off centerline to port. I could see water coming up under pressure. I couldn't help but think of submarine movies after the depth charge hits.

I reported this crack to the cutter helmsman. He said to monitor it and let him know if it worsened. I asked whether I should try caulking it with something, though I didn't think I had anything that would cure on a wet surface. He said sure, try it.

So I went through our supplies and found 3M 4200, a caulking compound I knew would not cure and would not be up to the job. That was all I had, and it wasn't worth trying. I hadn't really counted on cracks in the hull. I had assumed that the integrity of the steel hull, as long as I kept it coated to prevent corrosion, would be the one thing on this boat I could always count on. It was ABS Marine Grade A steel, the best steel you can use for a boat, welded using proper techniques and equipment, and inspected by Bureau Veritas, an international classification society. If you can't count on that, why bother with any of the rest? All the other work I had done on the boat didn't really make sense if the hull wasn't going to stay in one piece.

I tried to reassure Nancy, because she looked worried. I guess being fifty miles from land in thousands of feet of water at night in stormy conditions being yanked through the water at nine knots by a group of incompetents while we had a crack in our hull somehow gave her cause for concern.

"Steel doesn't really tear," I said. "Not like how a crack could open up in a cement, wood, or fiberglass hull. The molecules are flexible, you know, like how you can melt a metal into a liquid. I remember this from chemistry. The cell walls in wood are rigid and can crack, but steel shouldn't do that. So it should be okay to have a crack, and it shouldn't be able to rip apart any of the rest of the hull."

This explanation was pretty much incoherent, and certainly desperate and inaccurate, but Nancy seemed willing to accept it, at least for now, since there wasn't much other encouragement I could offer.

By around 4 A.M., we could see the lights of St. Croix, and by daybreak we were being towed into a big bay protected from waves. We anchored, then began a long search by radio for yards that could repair us. We finally found St. Croix Marine, a boatyard on the other side of the island. They agreed to an emergency haulout, so Nancy and I picked up anchor and found that we could steer fine in calm conditions. But then, when we were halfway there, cruising along the northern coast, St. Croix Marine canceled the haul because their railway had rust and they were afraid our hundred-ton boat might break it.

I was feeling desperate, since we were now underway, leaking with a crack in our hull, and had nowhere to go for repairs. Nancy came up from below looking oddly happy with her mop and bucket, getting the boat all cleaned up for our charter, keeping the aft bilge water low, and I hated to tell her the news.

"How can they do that?" she asked. "Don't they know we have a crack in our hull?"

"I know," I said. "I'm trying to find other options."

"Well what are the other options?"

"I don't have any yet."

"Oh great," she said, and went back below to pump the bilge again.

After many more calls on the radio, I came up with one last option, a salvage diver in the British Virgin Islands who had a good reputation and lots of experience. He had done underwater rudder repair for many boats, including removing a rudder, taking it to the shop, then reinstalling it. So I turned to port, my beam to the waves, and sailed away from St. Croix.

The steering was easy, but I tried to baby the rudder as much as possible, not putting any force on it. It was a beautiful day, sunny and bright, only a few scattered squalls, none of them in our path. The seas built to five or six feet, so that we rolled slightly in the troughs, but it wasn't bad.

After about two hours, Nancy reported that the water from the crack was coming in at an increased rate, so I went below to check. The water was sloshing back and forth, as it had before, since we were rolling a bit. The pump was still faster than the leak, but not by a lot. Luckily, we were only an hour and a half from our rendezvous point.

I returned to the helm. "I'm glad we're meeting the diver soon," I told Nancy.

Then we heard a loud metallic sound in the stern and the boat went into a spin. I turned the helm but there was no response. I pulled back on the throttles.

"There's water in the hallway," Nancy said from down in the main salon. "There's too much water for the pump."

I went below for a quick look. The hallway was flooding, already a few feet deep. I knew from our spinning that we had lost our rudder. And I knew from this water suddenly in the hallway that the rudder had taken a piece of our hull with it.

"Grab our ditch bag," I told Nancy. "And get our important papers from the desk. We're abandoning ship." I went for the radio.

"MAYDAY, MAYDAY, MAYDAY," I called on channel 16. "This is the sailing vessel *Bird of Paradise,* the sailing vessel *Bird of Paradise*. We have lost our rudder and are flooding and sinking fast. We are at 18 degrees 9.2 North, 64 degrees 39.8 West, approximately 10 miles south of Norman Island. That's one eight degrees nine decimal two North, six four degrees three nine decimal eight West, approx ten miles south of Norman Island. We are two persons on board, two adults, David Vann and Nancy Flores. Vessel is ninety feet, white hull, two wooden masts, wooden pilothouse. This is a MAYDAY, MAYDAY, MAYDAY. We are sinking fast."

"I have your disk with your writing," Nancy said, holding my red backup disk. "What else do you want?"

"Did you grab all the papers out of the drawer?"

"Yeah. What else?"

"Put a life jacket on. And first, can you grab my black folding knife? I need it to cut the dinghy free."

Virgin Islands Search and Rescue (VISAR) hailed me on the

radio. They acknowledged the mayday and asked again for my position. They said they had a twenty-two-foot rescue boat responding. I gave my position again.

"Can you also raise your mainsail?" the controller asked.

"Why?" I asked.

"So the rescue boat can spot you more easily."

This was not a good idea. Our mainsail was huge and took a long time to put up. And it would make us heel over further and also push us forward through the water, even with the boom out. And the boom would be swinging as we rolled. I couldn't think of a worse suggestion. I didn't want to sound rude, though, since they were coming out to rescue us.

"Sorry," I said. "I'm not going to be able to do that. I need the time to cut the dinghy free." Then I left the radio. Maybe I should have gone for the small, light inflatable dinghy on our aft deck. It was tied with only one line, which would have been easy to remove. But I went for the larger dinghy, hanging off the davits on the stern. It was bigger and far more stable, and new. It had our boat name on it and would be easier to spot. But it was also 350 pounds, a fiberglass hull with inflatable tubes, so it was more difficult to manage.

I untied the lines that were keeping it from swaying back and forth, and as soon as I did that, it swayed hard. We were rolling even in the little six-foot waves, and we were also heeling strangely from the water coming in below, the stern sinking first. Then I unfastened a clip on the bow that was difficult to reach. I swung a bit as we rolled on a wave, and I was out over the water, my feet kicking in the air.

Nancy yelled at me to be careful. I freed the clip and got my feet back on deck. Then I loosened the reels that held the main davit lines, and they spun out dangerously, like fishing reel handles running free. That dropped the dinghy into the water, but each time our hull came up on a wave the dinghy was yanked by the davit lines. So I cut the davit lines, which put me out over the water again, and pulled the dinghy around toward the side boarding ladder.

The boat was heeling far over to port as it sank, because of the open porthole we'd used for the bilge pump, which meant that the boarding ladder on the starboard side was high out of the water and getting higher, with Nancy on it. She threw in the paddles and then she was ready to jump, but her jump was going to be five or six feet at least, and if she missed, she'd be in the water.

"Stop!" I yelled. "This is wrong. Too dangerous. I'll bring it around to the other side."

I pulled the dinghy aft, but the waves were yanking it from me. I was having a difficult time controlling its two short lines, afraid I would lose them and we'd have no dinghy. Then I thought I should let VISAR know we were abandoning ship, so I tried to wrap the lines around the starboard mizzen shroud, one of our steel rigging wires, and asked Nancy to hold them.

As soon as I left her, though, I could tell she wasn't going to be able to hold on. I ran back to her and tied the lines around the wire.

The radio, when I got to it at the helm, was dead. The system must have shorted out because of the flooding. The boat was getting low in the water, especially the port stern, and it was heeling over and wallowing in sick ways.

"The radio's dead," I told Nancy. "Hopefully they're coming for us."

I tried to untie the lines for the dinghy, but they were constantly yanked. A black nylon line and a blue sheathed polyester line. The blue line was for the bow, the most important, but I had to cut both lines to get them free, and that left the black line the longest. I remember staring at the colors, blue and black, feeling a bit confused, the knife seeming to take an awfully long time to cut through, the huge boat beneath me sagging like an old horse on its haunches, the deck getting steeper. When I finally sawed through, I grabbed the black line and just held on. The blue line was in the water.

I pulled the dinghy aft to the stern. I had meant to make it all the way around to the port side, because that's where Nancy was waiting with the ditch bag, but I realized I might not make it there in time. And the rail beside her was almost in the water, instead of ten feet off the water, as it should have been. The boat was going to sink to port, so if we tried to get into the dinghy there, the boat might roll over onto us.

"We're going off the stern!" I yelled to Nancy.

"The stern?" she yelled. "Where?" She was panicking, finally, as the boat went down.

"Over here!" I yelled. "Right here!" She was only twenty feet from me, but there was all this stuff in her way on the aft deck: a big fifty-five-horse outboard motor, heavy and dangerous; a green kayak filled with four heavy dive tanks; our enormous round white fenders, over fifty pounds each; our extra chain spilled out onto the teak from its bucket; boards and paddles and other gear. I was suddenly very afraid she might not be able to climb over all of it, afraid the boat could roll over right then and I'd lose her.

I was having a difficult time holding the dinghy, too, the black line yanking hard in my hands as I watched her come toward me. "Drop the life jackets!" I yelled. "Just get over here!"

She looked confused, but she dropped the two extras she was holding, held on to the ditch bag, and made it to me. Then she was ready to jump into the dinghy.

I tried to time it with the waves, waited until a wave brought the dinghy up close to us. "Okay, jump!" The dinghy fell away, and Nancy fell down farther than I had wanted, onto her knees, but she made it.

"I'm all right!" she yelled.

"Okay, scoot forward!" Our deck was dipping lower on each wave, until when I finally jumped, our stern was only a few inches off the water. In the summer, kids on one of the charters had jumped off the stern over and over, squealing in delight because it was so high.

I grabbed a paddle. Nancy was just looking at the boat.

"We have to paddle," I said. "We can't be near it when it sinks. We could get hit by a mast or the davits, and it may create suction when it goes down."

We worked hard to pull away from the stern. We just kept going until we were about a hundred yards away, then we heard a helicopter coming in fast, the U.S. Coast Guard.

The helicopter hovered directly over us, about fifty feet in the air. There was a guy in a jumpsuit hanging out the side with his thumb up, asking us, I supposed, if we were okay. So I put my thumb up to say we were all right.

The stern of our boat was getting lower as it rocked in the waves, the bow sticking up. It looked beautiful, the new cream-colored paint, the new varnish on the rails and pilot-house, the name in wedding script on the bows, the dark blue bottom paint. It was a gorgeous boat. Nancy found the digital camera in the ditch bag and snapped a couple of photos.

The helicopter had been circling and came in close now, approaching from downwind. They had something dangling in a plastic case.

"It must be a radio," I told Nancy. "We're supposed to catch it."

I held my hands up, showing I was ready to catch, and Nancy did the same. Having my hands up made me realize how much we were getting rocked in the waves. I had to put one hand down to hold on.

The helicopter brought the radio right to me, the pilot impressive.

The Coast Guard wanted to know if anyone else was onboard, and I reassured them no one was. They said the VISAR rescue boat would arrive in about twenty minutes, and I told them we could wait. They said there was also a cutter on its way, and a merchant vessel. I could see the merchant vessel a few miles east of us. It was huge. I didn't want to be rescued by the cutter or the merchant vessel. I knew from getting on the freighter in Moroccan waters how dangerous it can be to board a big ship in waves.

"This is *Bird of Paradise*," I called on the radio. "We would like to be rescued by VISAR. We do not want to try to board the cutter or the merchant vessel. I repeat, we request rescue in the smaller, twenty-two-foot VISAR boat, because it will be much safer and easier."

I didn't hear a response. There were a lot of conversations about us on channel 16, the voices overlapping, all of them difficult for me to hear: VISAR, the Coast Guard helicopter, Coast Guard San Juan, the Coast Guard cutter, the merchant vessel, and maybe even a salvage company. Coast Guard San Juan was giving an ETA for the cutter arrival, VISAR was giving its ETA to Coast Guard San Juan, and the Coast Guard helicopter was going back and forth with the merchant vessel, trying to get it to stay farther away. It was threatening to run us over, heading straight at us from upwind.

Our boat was sinking fast. Within five minutes after we had abandoned ship, it was taking large rolls to port, and the stern was beginning to submerge. The smaller inflatable dinghy was floating up off the aft deck, as were the large white fenders.

"I can't believe this is happening," Nancy said.

"Look at it," I said. "It's sinking. It's actually going down."

Nancy took more photos. The bow went up until the top of the mizzenmast was touching the water behind the boat. Then it fell to the side, and various items floated off the aft deck. "Take more pictures," I said, then I looked at Nancy and saw the cap was on the lens. "The cap is still on the lens," I said.

"Oh, sorry," she said.

It was oddly normal, watching our boat sink. We watched it roll and tip and then the bow and its cream-colored bowsprit were pointing straight into the sky, the back half of the boat completely submerged. The mainmast, all ninety feet of it, was lying out parallel just above the surface of the water. The mizzenmast and pilothouse were already gone. The varnish on the railing looked perfect. The white Italian windlass was bolted solidly in the middle of the teak deck. Everything intact, even the rigging. I realized I should never have worried about the masts. They were solid. The boat was probably much better than I had ever trusted it to be, except, of course, for the rudder, its Achilles' heel.

This was the first time I had looked at the varnish and paint and not worried about it. There would be no more maintenance, no more work. I was done. There was an odd sense of relief.

"That's our boat," Nancy said.

"It looks so beautiful," I said.

"It does," she said. "We finally had it fixed up. We were going to make it."

The bow fell to port, rose up again only partially, then a large wave hid our view, and when it had cleared, our boat was gone.

The life raft popped up, inflating fast. It was huge, a raft for twenty people, orange and black, like a Doughboy pool floating out on the ocean. There were a lot of other items on the water, too: our other dinghy, boards that had fit over seats, cushions, a mattress, extra life jackets and life rings.

The helicopter reported that our boat had sunk. They said they would drop a smoke flare just downwind to help VISAR spot us, and we watched as they circled and dropped the smoke. I radioed to let them know I had smoke canisters, if they wanted me to light one closer, but they said I didn't need to. They were focused mostly on the merchant ship, which was now very near. They had told it to turn away and keep a good distance from us, but it kept coming.

Then Nancy spotted one of our CD cases floating by. "Let's grab it," I said, so we paddled hard, got up close, and it disappeared. We had run over it, sinking it. But then we saw a paddle drifting by and were able to grab that. It was the debris game, oddly fun in our shocked state.

The merchant vessel seemed confused in its responses over the radio, so the Coast Guard helicopter left us to go talk to it. I'm not sure why they couldn't have stayed, since they were using their radio, but as soon as they left, two unusually large waves hit us. Nancy was in the middle of the dinghy, holding on to the side ropes with both hands, but I was up in the bow paddling, so when the second wave flipped us, I was thrown out of the dinghy into the water.

I felt a sharp pain where my knee had banged hard against the fiberglass and twisted. I was underwater, and tumbling, but my eyes were open and I happened to see the blue and white bow line flying past me. I reached out and caught it with my left hand, was yanked to the surface by the force of the dinghy getting blown downwind, and saw Nancy standing in the dinghy, yelling my name. Her face looked terrible. If nothing else, I felt loved and missed.

"I'm okay!" I yelled. "I'm here!" She looked around to both sides, then forward and finally saw me. She leaned over the bow, yelling my name, and started pulling in the line. I held on with one hand and swam with the other. I came around the side and pulled myself up on the handles, back into the dinghy. I just held on to Nancy for a moment, happy to be safe, then I worried about the possibility of other big waves and grabbed a paddle.

"Well," I said. "That was nice."

"I couldn't find you," she said.

"I banged my knee," I told her. "I think it's hurt."

I paddled us around until we were facing the swells again, then I grabbed the radio, which had stayed in the bottom of the boat with our ditch bag and other stuff. It had been such a fast flip that I was the only thing to go overboard, other than the paddle I'd been holding.

"Our dinghy just flipped," I reported on 16. "This is *Bird of Paradise*. Our dinghy just flipped and I was thrown overboard. I got back in, but my knee was banged, and we can't stay out here long. We need to be rescued soon."

I didn't receive any response to this message. Everyone was so busy in their arrangements. I assumed they had heard, though, and that they were coming as fast as they could.

"Let's paddle for the life raft," told Nancy. "That will be safer, in case they take a while. It's more stable."

We paddled hard for the raft and passed downwind of it but managed to get back upwind and reach its boarding ladder.

I helped Nancy get in first, threw our ditch bag, then climbed in myself, holding the dinghy's bow line. I was tying the line to our raft when Nancy yelled that she saw the rescue boat from VISAR. I kept tying, so that the dinghy and life raft would be together, but I looked up and was grateful to see the orange tubes of their hard-bottomed inflatable glide by.

There were three guys on board. They came around upwind of us so that their side tube lay against the life raft, and I helped Nancy get in, then the ditch bag, then I got in. My knee really hurt when I lifted it over the tube.

"I banged my knee," I told them.

"We'll get you taken care of," one of them said. They were busy clipping us in so that we couldn't fall overboard. The Coast Guard helicopter was overhead, one of the crew members hanging out the side taking photos of us.

Then we were off, and the ride was fun. Nancy and I were in good spirits. I talked far too much, going on and on about how happy we were to be alive, how I had been thinking of joining VISAR myself, how I couldn't believe the boat had sunk, all the work we had done, etc. I was a mess. It seemed to me at the time that I was handling it well, maintaining good perspective in the face of tragedy, but I see now that I was just a mess. In shock and elated from surviving.

This good mood continued in both of us for several days. When we first arrived in Roadtown, a clothing store gave us a hundred-dollar gift certificate. I was wearing only a life jacket, shorts, and Tevas, so it was nice to get a dry pair of shorts and a shirt. Nancy was grateful for a skirt and blouse.

Then we were checked into a hotel for free and given dinner for free at their restaurant. Nancy and I were amazed. Everyone was so generous. And this continued the next day with free services from a notary and even a lawyer.

At some point, though, the elation had to end.

My THIRTY-FIFTH BIRTHDAY was three days after the boat sank. We had dinner at the marina restaurant. All the few faces we knew were there, but we were sitting at our own table, and no one came over to say hello. I could tell they were already tired of us. It had been an exciting, tragic event that had warranted some degree of ceremony and many acts of kindness in the first two days, but now it was day three and it would be better if we could move along. We hadn't been here long enough to become friends with anyone, and we no longer represented business with our big boat. We were becoming dead weight.

The restaurant had a live local band playing Clapton and Jimmy Buffet songs. We splurged, having a Bushwhacker first, then BBQ chicken and ribs. I held a bag of ice on my knee. We talked of California and still getting out on the water. Michael, who had bought *Grendel,* would take us sailing on the bay.

A large sloop was coming in, its navigation lights and lower spreaders lit. It was a beautiful, expensive boat, not nearly as big as ours, but probably seventy feet. It was moving slowly, all its fenders out, down the fairway between docks A and B. There was a gusty wind, as usual, so they'd be exposed and sliding sideways in the fairway, but they would turn upwind into their slip, which would make it easy. Even with the wind right, though, I had never relaxed. It was too much weight, with too many possible surprises and too little power to control. I didn't think I would miss big boats. Maybe small powerboats were the right thing. Nancy was always joking about boats small enough you can stick out an arm or a leg at the dock if you're coming in too fast. That sounded good. Enjoyment on the water not spoiled by fear.

But that night, after we'd returned to our hotel room and I watched *Overboard,* an '80s movie with Goldie Hawn and Kurt Russell, as Nancy slept, I felt so lost. I couldn't even tell exactly what it was. I was thirty-five, and I had come close to escaping everything I wanted to escape. We'd had charters to look forward to, money coming in, the boat finally fixed and ready. We were escaping the middle class, which is really the working class. And the only thing that could have prevented our escape was some extreme event. I'd had this thought several times in the past six months—that only something extreme could stop us now. And then it had. An unforecasted storm combining a tropical wave with an upper-level low hit us with force 11, just short of a hurricane, and we sank a mile down, in just over five thousand feet of water. Even if the insurance paid, nearly everything would go to my lenders, who certainly would not offer the loans again. So we had no way back. It was difficult to believe.

Work so that you can keep working. I had wanted to escape this. In the summer, as we enjoyed our honeymoon in the islands and it seemed all would turn out well, I had felt that being a captain and business owner lacked dignity and engagement and was therefore no dream at all. I wanted to return to the university. But this return was dependent upon financial freedom. I hadn't appreciated at the time that financial freedom itself is a worthy dream. Now, in my efforts to free myself from the working world, I had made myself a bankrupt, racked up more than $60,000 on my wife's credit cards, which would probably force her into bankruptcy, and left the university, my former career, long enough I would not be able to return. I had trapped myself and my wife in the working world so firmly we'd have to take any jobs we could get.

I had also wanted to escape cheap apartments. They had always depressed me. But now even this would be out of my reach, because I wouldn't be able to pass a credit check, and neither would Nancy. I would have to live with Nancy at her parents' house for now, and I didn't know when that would end.

But there was something more, some general, hollow ache I couldn't name. I just felt lost. Everything had been decimated, mostly through my own blind workings but also by what felt like a powerful fate—hubris, perhaps—a force swelling like an enormous wave and crashing upon me, making me see the world would not be shaped by my will. Like Oedipus, I had run and run and escaped nothing. And what had happened could not be undone. Who I had been before could never be returned to me. The only word I could think of was *ruin*.

And most likely it would get worse. The insurance could refuse to pay because I had moved the boat from a safe harbor in St. Croix toward the British Virgin Islands in my attempt to find repair. Then there was Nancy's impending bankruptcy. And my lenders might sue. They could obtain judgments against me and attach my wages.

I had already been threatened by the broker who had booked five charters for us and helped us in so many ways. He wanted his broker's commissions on the four canceled charters. He said he had earned these commissions, and it's true he had worked hard for them. But he wanted to put a lien on my insurance policy. This would only delay and complicate my already difficult claim.

"These clients will want their money back, David. How are they going to be paid?"

I had to take a hard line. I told him the insurance would not pay for loss of business, especially a third party's loss of business.

"So you're telling me to stuff it. After all I've done for you."

"No, I'm just saying the boat sank, I have no money and no job, and the insurance will not cover your commission."

"After all I've done for you. I am ashamed of David Vann. I am ashamed of the day I first heard the name David Vann."

"Did you hear that we lost our boat?" I asked.

"I am ashamed of the name David Vann. I am going to have to put my lawyer on you."

"Go ahead," I said. "Your contract says right in it that you give up the right to sue under the contract."

"Oh, so that's how it is. After all I've done for you. I am ashamed of the name David Vann."

MY FATHER KILLED himself in his new, unfurnished house in Fairbanks, Alaska, alone and suffering. It may have been a beautiful scene outside, the long stands of paper birch etched in moonlight or even the green, wavering bands of northern lights, since it was winter. But what he did was bitter and small and left us with two mysteries.

One is the mystery of his life and suicide, sealed forever. The other, abiding in each of us who loved him, is the impossibility of knowing or living the life we would have had without his suicide. Would I have thrown away my academic career—and, for a time, my writing—for boats and the sea if my father had not killed himself? Have I built boats out of love or obedience? The questions are impossible to answer. My own reasons are an opaque sea, my own dreams and desires things I can never fully know. I can only hope that my entire life hasn't been a plaything of his abrupt end.

In any case, like my father I've built my life around boats, and a boat builder is part of who I've become. Two years after the sinking, I've gone back into business with new partners and am nearing completion of a ninety-foot aluminum sailing catamaran, *Paradiso*. I've designed every part of *Paradiso*, every curve and line, and I've been at the warehouse every day to build it. All of that aluminum, so similar to watching my father's boat being built.

A year ago, even before we had welded the first plates, I could see it three-dimensionally in my head, from any vantage, from within any stateroom. Its flybridge, open to the sun and stars, has a teak deck and more than two hundred square feet of cushions. This is the excitement for me, the creation of something from nothing, the pre-existence of form, and the constant modification, also, the reshaping every day as I refine the design. Even metal is as malleable as a manuscript.

The boat is unique. It will be the largest sailing catamaran based in the Virgin Islands, and it is one of the largest ever built in the United States. Inspected and certified by the Coast Guard, it far exceeds even their regulations, with each hull divided into nine separate watertight compartments. There have been many hassles during construction, and no doubt these will continue, but in three weeks we will launch, and a week later I will sail with Nancy and my uncle and friends from San Francisco to Panama and then to the Virgin Islands on a ship of my own creation, a beautiful bird with wings.

A life can be like a work of art, constantly melted away and reshaped. The imagining and remaking is itself a form of satisfaction, especially when I'm dreaming together with Nancy. And this is what I wish my father had known. Many of his dreams ended in ruin, but his mistake was in not waiting for the new dreams to arrive, and in not realizing that those dreams were to be shared. He could have been nearly anything, his life reshapable in thousands of ways, none of which he, or those of us who still love him, will ever know.

Acknowledgments

MY DEEPEST THANKS to John L'Heureux, mentor and friend for more than fifteen years. Thanks, also, to Charlie Junkerman, who has always been unreasonably generous.

Thanks to Mike Curtis at the *Atlantic Monthly* for publishing my first short story, which opened many doors, Noah Lukeman, who has been a tireless agent, and Jofie Ferrari-Adler at Thunder's Mouth Press, a fabulous editor.

I will always be indebted to the creative writing program at Stanford University, where I was an undergraduate, Wallace Stegner Fellow, John L'Heureux Fellow, Jones Lecturer, and Continuing Studies Lecturer, and to the creative writing program at Cornell University, where I received my MFA. In particular, I must thank Stephanie Vaughn and Robert Morgan at Cornell, and John and Joan L'Heureux, Ken Fields, Simone DiPiero, Toby Wolff, Eavan Boland, Michelle Carter, Laura Selznick, Leslie Cahoon, Shirley Heath, Adrienne Rich, and Grace Paley at Stanford.

Many thanks, also, to the writers who were kind enough to

endorse my book, with a special thanks to Melanie Thern-strom, Keith Scribner, Jason Brown, and especially Julie Hilden for encouragement, advice, and inspiration.

Thank you to friends Jeff and Lora Colflesh, Margie and Pete Wilkinson, Dave O'Rourke, Michael Pardee, Mark Martinek, Steve Toutonghi, Forrest Melton, Craig Triplett, John Romano, Hilary Hug, Cristal Guderjahn, Shalini Mehan, Paula Moya, Gita Srinivasan, Zaidi Langworthy, Galen Palmer, my father-in-law and mother-in-law Salvador and Ofie Flores, and Pat and Jeff Saturnio. And thank you, finally, to my mother and the other women in my family who have always supported my writing, ever since the early stories about squirrels; to my uncle Doug, who crossed oceans with me three times; and to my wife Nancy, who endured everything and managed somehow to remain happy and loving.